CHRISTIANS ALIVE

Handbook
for
Spiritual Growth
•
edited by
Cliff Pederson

AUGSBURG PUBLISHING HOUSE

Minneapolis, Minnesota

ACKNOWLEDGEMENTS

A special thank you to all who wrote the articles included in this book. Through their personal friendship God has brought growth to my life.

Love and thanksgiving to God for my wife, Janelle. She loves me, keeps pace with me, and daily is God's instrument of peace.

CHRISTIANS ALIVE

Copyright © 1973 Augsburg Publishing House

Library of Congress Catalog Card No. 73-78259

International Standard Book No. 0-8066-1324-5

᾿

Scripture quotations unless otherwise noted are from the Revised Standard Version (RSV), copyright 1946 and 1952 by the Division of Christian Education of the National Council of Churches; from *The New English Bible* (NEB) copyright 1961 by Oxford University Press; from *The New Testament in Modern English* (Phillips) copyright 1958 by J. B. Phillips; from The Living Bible (LB) copyright 1971 by Tyndale House Publishers; and from The New American Standard Bible, copyright 1960, 1962, 1963 by The Lockman Foundation, are used by permission.

Manufactured in the United States of America.

CHRISTIANS ALIVE

ALIVE TO THE WORLD

Preface

As you open this book, *Christians Alive*, I have two thoughts I want to leave with you. One thought may be characterized as "bad news," the other as "good news."

First the *bad news*. This book will not bring instant maturity to your Christian life. If you are looking for 10 easy steps to maturity, spiritual renewal in 21 chapters, then you've wasted your money and you will be wasting your time. There is no cram course for Christian maturity. Maturity is the combination of inner devotion, outward service, intellectual integrity, and time. And there is no short-cut.

Many people do not want to dedicate themselves to a life-long maturing process. They are part of the "now generation." They want everything either now or yesterday. This attitude affects us all to some degree. We are all part of the instant, freeze-dried, self-service, pre-packaged, pop-up, pre-fabricated age.

The books we buy often reflect this attitude. We diligently search through shelves of books picking those that promise easy answers and quick results: *Automobile Repair Made Easy, Learn to Sew Overnight, Five Simple Steps to Financial Security, The Ease of Cooking, Lose Weight Without Trying, Investment Tips that Never Fail, Learn French While You Sleep.*

Christians Alive does not fall in this category . . . and that's the *good news*. We are not offering these articles to you as a condensed form of Christian maturity. *Christians Alive* is not a spiritual reader's digest.

The 21 articles in this book should not be viewed as your final destination, but rather as your point of departure. Your goal should not be to *recite* the points made in these articles, but rather to *reflect* in your life the great truths of Scripture presented here.

Some of you who are reading these words are new Christians. You have recently come to faith in Jesus Christ. Welcome to the family! Let me share with you a personal experience. When I first became consciously aware of God's love for me through Christ, I wanted to understand more about God, His Word, His church. The first subject that came to my attention concerned the *future*. Future happenings, things to come captured my thoughts. I read everything I could understand on the subject and then some. In short I was a future freak. In my haste to learn about the future, I neglected the past and the present. I became a one-sided, lop-sided individual. My Christian life was off-balance because I had not taken time to lay a broad foundation.

Christians Alive offers you the opportunity of laying a broad foundation. You do not have to stumble off-balance through life, ricocheting from one extreme to another—from rapid growth to dormant stagnation. You came to life through Christ, you can stay alive through Christ—and it's all God's provision. He has provided for our maturity. It is God who remakes us daily to conform to the image of his Son.

You will not be magically mature after reading these articles. That's the bad news. You will begin to lay a broad foundation for your daily growth. That's the good news. And God is the author of all good news.

Cliff Pederson

Oswald C. J.
Hoffmann

The
Way
of
Salvation

When you are really sick, you want to find a real cure. If you are bothered by a minor ailment, you might experiment with home-remedies and patent medicines. But when your life is at stake, you settle for nothing less than the best and surest cure. It may be that you will consult two or three doctors in order to find out what is wrong with you. At a time like that, you don't suppose for a moment that all medicines are equally good. You'd be very impatient with anyone who said, "It doesn't make any difference what treatment you take. The main thing is that you are sincere."

When you are seriously ill, the wrong remedy might make you even sicker. That's why you're so cautious and can't afford to make a mistake—it might mean death for you.

Being sick, and realizing that you are sick, are often two different things. Not being aware of the fact that you are sick doesn't make you any better. It just puts off the evil day, and it may also prevent you from seeking the opportunity to be cured while the opportunity is there.

THE DIAGNOSIS

In writing this article and in my weekly preaching I have the unpleasant duty to tell the world that it is sick, sick unto death because it has left its God behind. I have the unpleasant duty to tell people that because they are sick, they must seek a cure. At the same time, I have the glorious privilege of telling the whole world that there is a cure, that God Himself has reached out in love and mercy in order to heal the souls of men.

St. Peter healed a man who had been lame from his birth with the simple words: *"Silver and gold have I none, but such as I have give I thee. In the name of Jesus Christ of Nazareth rise up and walk"* (Acts 3:6 KJV). When the Apostle was cross-examined because of this miracle-working power that had been given to him, he preached nothing more or less than the *name* of Jesus Christ of Nazareth. He said to the rulers, elders, and scribes, the high-priests who were gathered together to hear him: *"Be it known unto you all, and to all the people of Israel, that by the name of Jesus Christ of Nazareth, whom ye crucified, whom God raised from the dead, even by Him doth this man stand here before you whole. . . . Neither is there salvation in any other; for there is none other name under heaven given among men, whereby we must be saved"* (Acts 4:10-12 KJV).

As that one lame man stood before the whole assemblage, healthy and saved, so each one of us can enjoy safety by believing in the name of Jesus Christ. This is not some magic that Peter is talking about here.

It is real healing, coming from the Giver of life Himself. It is healing of the whole man, both body and soul; it is healing for time and for eternity.

Salvation means spiritual recovery; it means being restored to health, to the kind of wholeness which God intended a man to have, both in his relations to God and in his relations to his fellowmen.

In this text Peter tells us where we can find this salvation, this wholeness. He insists that there is only one cure in all the world for the spiritual ailments that afflict mankind. That cure, he says, is to be found in the name of Jesus Christ. A lot of people say that it doesn't make any difference where you look for salvation, for healing of the spirit. These people claim that one religion is just as good as the other, and that the only important thing is that you are sincere.

To people like this Peter says politely, but firmly, "I'm afraid that you're terribly wrong. There is salvation in no one else, for there is no other name under heaven given among men by which we must be saved." As we think about the implications of this statement, we are going to see the sense and the beauty of it. We are going to see how important it is that we apply Christ's cure to our needs.

THE SICKNESS

All the spiritual ills of mankind can be lumped together in one word. That word is *"sin."* The better we understand the general disease, which is sin, the better will we understand individual spiritual ailments that afflict each one of us. What is it that makes a person sick? Well, a person becomes sick when some germ or poison or malignancy gets into his system and begins to attack his body. Sickness is a sort of invasion by a destructive force.

Sin works the same way. You can see the symptoms of the disease in your heart and in your life. There are the wrongs that we do, sometimes in spite of the fact that we don't want to do them. There are the things that we say, for which we could cut off our tongues after we have said them. There are the thoughts that we think, which later cause us to wonder whatever made them come into our minds.

This happens to all of us, whether we are rich or poor, whether we are intelligent or simpleminded. All of us have been guilty at one time or another of doing wrong to God. It may be by ignoring Him, by disobeying Him, by taking His name in vain, or perhaps by just failing to trust Him as we should. The wrong spreads at the time to other people. We hurt them, we irritate them, we despise them, we insult them. Think of the thousands and thousands of wrongs that you have done in your lifetime. Each one of them is a symptom, a sign, that you are infected by the disease of sin, which is constantly trying to destroy you spiritually.

THE REMEDY

Peter put all of these wrongs together when he said that in Jesus Christ there is salvation, salvation from sin. Christ came into the world with the dedicated purpose of rescuing mankind from its ills. As He looked upon sinful people, His heart ached with pity and He was determined to do something to help us. He wanted to heal us of our sins, and then to protect us against future attacks.

To accomplish this, He took the deadly force of sin

into His own Body on the tree of the cross. Though He was innocent of sin Himself, though sin could never tempt Him successfully, Christ injected the deadly virus of sin into His own Person. On the cross He suffered the most violent death that sin could possibly bring about. Not only was He rejected by men, He was also forsaken by God. Everything happened to Him that happens to a man who is loaded with sin.

He did all of this voluntarily, like a courageous scientist, who is so determined to reach his goal that he will inject the deadly germs into his own veins. The difference between Christ and the scientist, of course, was that He was not just out to prove something, but to do something for us. He did all of this for us.

When the disease of sin had done its worst damage, taken Him down to death and even to damnation, He recovered again with the sweeping victory of the resurrection. And now He stands alive and strong, ready to rescue us from sin, too. He can share His victory over sin with each one of us. His blood, with its healing power, is the antibiotic, the healing and immunizing serum that makes us victors over sin. For in His blood there is redemption. It was a bloody sacrifice that He brought, but that's what it took to overcome sin, even as Isaiah said: *"By His stripes we are healed."*

NO OTHER NAME

This is why there is salvation in Jesus Christ and in Him only. He struggled with sin and came out victorious over it—in His own Body, in His own Mind, in His own Spirit. He suffered with our sin and survived it. No one else has ever done this. No other religion describes or offers healing of this kind. That is why Christ stands alone in His glory, why Christ alone is the crowned Son of the eternal God, why He demands our faith and commands our devotion, why there is salvation in no other name, than in the Name of Jesus Christ.

NO OTHER SALVATION

I know there are people who object when you tell them that only in Christ can salvation be found. They say, "You mean that God is so narrow and so exclusive as to make Christ the only Way? Don't you think His love is big enough to include all the religions, all the ways of salvation that men have believed in?"

That objection is not as convincing as it sounds. Of course, God's love is big. It actually does reach out to all mankind. He is wise enough and powerful enough to do whatever He wants. But the fact remains that His love and wishes and power all led Him to one great conclusion. In His love and wisdom and power He contrived the best possible cure for sin through the death of His Son, and He offers this cure to one and all without effort or payment of any kind.

It is not for us to tell God how to do things, to insist that He make other cures work just as well as the one He has provided. All He asks is that we accept His salvation in Jesus Christ. My friend, there is only one thing for you to do, and that is to accept Jesus Christ, humbly and gratefully, by faith. Reach out to Him as He reaches out to you. Take Him to yourself, and make Him your own! Do this as if your life depended on it. It does!

Roy Hendrickson

How Can I Know the Will of God?

The young man stepped through my office door, sat down and blurted out, "How can I find God's will for me?" He skipped any niceties of introduction; the question was flatly stated, and I was on the spot for an answer. He had been dropping in at church services for several months. He was not a member of our congregation, and he wasn't known for much religious interest.

My response was, "Do you have peace with God, whose will you are seeking?"

Again he answered flatly, "No." So we began by looking at what it meant to be in a relationship of faith in God, with forgiveness of sins through Jesus Christ.

We can spin our mental wheels furiously in seeking God's will and never move off dead center until we are established in an open relationship with God. Anything in life that blocks out open conversation with God (sin, selfishness, pride, bitterness), must be faced honestly and given up to Him. Only then can we be open to God. And only then can God make Himself known to us (Hebrews 12:1-2). This is the first step in knowing God's will.

UNANSWERED QUESTIONS

But suppose that this relationship of faith is open, and the Spirit of God witnesses with our spirit that we are children of God. There are still a lot of questions left unanswered. What about the future, a job, school, a girl or guy to date and perhaps marry? What is right for my occupation? Who is right for a life partner? What is God's will when I am with my friends? What about death at an early age, by accident or illness?

First, we must consider the possibility that using the term *God's will* can be a cop-out. We hear people who say about everything, "It is God's will," and they assume this releases them from responsibility.

A teen-ager dies in a fiery collision. A student flunks a course in algebra. A person is bypassed for a job promotion. A little child dies from eating prescription pills. A teen-ager feels left-out, ugly, put-down. Is each instance God's will? Could it be that the driver who caused the accident was stoned; the student never studied; the pills were carelessly left on the table; the teen-ager never accepted himself and projected this self-rejection to others, and then withdrew from them into a shell of loneliness? To attribute all these activities to God's will is to disregard human frailty, laziness, neglect, and the weakness of the flesh. God's will is never meant to be a cop-out.

To seek God's will honestly means we assume responsible relationships, actions, and attitudes as an integral part of life. In relationships, God's will is that we love one another as He loved us (John 13:34-35). In action, God's will is that we do all to His glory (Colossians 3:17). In attitudes, God's will is that we have the mind of Christ (Philippians 2:1-15).

GOD CREATED EVERYTHING GOOD

Four very important things are central in knowing God's will. First, *God created everything and said it was good* (Genesis 1:31). And our attitudes are conditioned by what we know of God's plan for creation. God was not ashamed of male and female. He was pleased with plant and animal life. He wanted the best for everything and everyone. Therefore, relationships between the sexes are meant to be enjoyed and cherished in God's order. The way we ought to treat nature is to conserve and keep it. This has deep implication for seeking a life partner and life occupation. We can use both our head (brains) and our heart (feelings), thankful for both in seeking God's will for our sexuality and our job.

WE LIVE FOR GOD'S GLORY

Second, God's primary purpose for us is to know that He chose and destined us in love to be His children through Jesus Christ and *to live for the praise of His glory* (Ephesians 1:5-12). With this fact as a guiding principle you can weigh your decisions for education and occupation by seeking to answer, "Will these things fit into God's primary purpose for me?" This will eliminate a lot of the garbage and clarify your every decision.

GOD WORKS THROUGH PEOPLE

Third, how is this purpose of God accomplished among people? God works primarily through people to make known His love and purpose for all men. He came in Jesus Christ in the flesh to make Himself known. Now He gives us the commission to share the news of Jesus Christ as Savior and Lord. He reaches through us to help others know His love. His will is that you, in word and action, make known the Father's love through your person.

SIX SPECIFIC GUIDELINES

Fourth, how can I determine the specific ways that God's will is revealed to me so I can be sure about the answers?

1. Since God works through people, do not hesitate to seek the counsel of Christian friends, family, pastors, and professional guidance counselors. There is validity in the advice of the ancient sage: *"Without counsel plans go wrong, but with many advisers they succeed"* (Proverbs 15:22 RSV).

2. Seek the guidance of Scripture in formulating the thought patterns of your mind. It is still true that, *"Your words are a flashlight to light the path ahead of me, and keep me from stumbling"* (Psalm 119:105 LB).

3. Prayer is an avenue wide open in talking with God. Try it, remembering that Jesus said, *"Ask, and it will be given you; seek, and you will find; knock, and it will be opened to you"* (Matthew 7:7 RSV).

4. Be assured that the Holy Spirit is actively working to reproduce Christ's life in you and teach you the truth.

16

5. Yield obediently to what you know is right—that which you are convinced is the proper action. Many times we struggle to find God's will when we are disobedient to His will that has already been revealed.

6. Give your talents, strengths, abilities a chance to be used in service of God and man. Knowing yourself and living out your own identity is a real, gutsy thing that happens day by day. Live openly, expectantly, and thankfully to God, and He will reveal the abundant and useful life to you.

God's will is not as mysterious as people make it to be. His plan for man is revealed in Scripture, actualized in Jesus Christ, vitalized through people in this world, and personalized in the daily life of committed Christians. You can count on God. Now start living out your life right where you are, because that's where **Christ wants to work through you.**

Alvin N. Rogness | Why Bother to Pray?

Can you change God's mind by praying to Him? Does He wait to hear from you before He will do anything for you? By putting pressure on Him through repeated prayers can you "force" God to do what He may not have wanted to do from the start?

JUST WHAT HAPPENS WHEN YOU PRAY?

There are people who say that the only thing that happens when you pray is that you feel better. Nothing changes as far as God is concerned. He loves you as much when you do not pray as when you do, so why bother to pray?

Other people say that prayer opens you up to God so that He can change you. If you do not pray, you keep the door shut to God's work within you. He wants to give you faith and hope and love. He can do this much more effectively if you will pray.

Still others believe that in some strange and unexplained way prayer opens the way for God to do more than just change you. Prayer opens the way for God to change circumstances, like stopping a war or a tornado.

One thing is sure. Since there is a God, He certainly would like to have you talk to Him. He wants communication and relationship. If you have a friend, it would be strange if you never talked to him or if you talked to him only when you wanted something from him.

PRAYER IS GETTING TO KNOW GOD

Perhaps that is the profoundest reason for praying—not in order to change God's mind, nor in order that He might change you, nor that He might change things, but simply that you and God might know one another and live with one another. God speaks to you through His Word; you speak to Him in prayer. Prayer opens the lines of communication. Prayer opens a fuller relationship with God.

Obviously, God wants to do things for you and with you. He wants for you only that which is good, and He knows better than you what that might be. He does not sit around, therefore, like a bell-hop waiting to run whatever errand you think up. He is God. He gives the orders. Prayer is probably a way to hear His commands rather than a way to give Him orders.

But it is not only His commands that He wants you to hear. Above all else, He wants you to know His love for you. To strike up a conversation with God (praying) is to learn of His amazing love. It is a way for

God to reinforce the wonderful story of His love in Christ which you find in the Scriptures.

PRAYER IS GOING TO YOUR FATHER

We dare not limit God, of course. He has told us to pray. He has assured that He hears our prayers. In fact, He puts no limits on what we might pray for or about. We can come to Him with the most trivial things, like passing a test or having someone fall in love with us, if these indeed are trivial. In any event, God is like a great and good Father. And any father is honored by having his child come to him for all sorts of things. The saddest thing for a father would be if his child no longer bothered to come to him at all.

God, our heavenly Father, does not want us to fight our battles alone. If we are in trouble, He is anxious to enter. If we are tripped up by temptations, He wants to lend us His strength. If we are weighed down by guilts, He wants to enter with His forgiveness to free us.

PRAYER IS GETTING THE BEST

Our prayers may not always be answered the way we might have hoped. But remember that God knows better than we what should be done. He will sort out our prayers and cancel out the ones that might do us harm. So that shouldn't stop us from praying for all sorts of things. God has our best interest in mind.

Also, God Himself may be blocked out from giving us what He wants us to have. Our own sinfulness or the sins of others may stand in his way. In this fallen world the power of evil with its tragedy, pain and death may keep God's will from being done. God suffers, as we suffer.

PRAYER IS SAYING "THANKS"

The finest kind of prayer is a prayer of thanksgiving. When you are through listing the things you want from God, try thanking Him for a long list of good things that He has given you. First on your list should be the great gift of life which He gave you through the cross of Jesus Christ. No matter what happens to you, this gift cannot be taken from you against your will.

SOME SPECIFIC SUGGESTIONS FOR PRAYING

First, *have some fixed times for prayer.* Be sure to join others in prayer when you can, either in small groups or certainly on Sunday when the congregation gathers to thank God.

Lean heavily on "helps," like the Psalms or books that contain great prayers. To be left to ourselves alone is to miss some of the great things that we ought to have in our prayers.

Pray for others, your family, your pastors and leaders in the church, the leaders of governments. Keep in mind the people who are suffering. And, having prayed for them, seek ways of being God's agents to help them.

Above all, *remember that you have a right to go directly to God* because He has created you to be His child. In Christ Jesus (your Savior, Lord, and Brother) you are a restored son or daughter of the everlasting Kingdom. You are a child of the King. His treasures are yours—yours for the asking.

Don Williams

The
Bible
in Your
Life

What is the Bible for you? A museum piece? A family scrapbook? Rules and regulations?

The Bible is an exciting love story, a magnificent adventure, a source of life and power. The Bible moves from creation to consummation. It is dominated by great personalities who lived boldly in the light of God through several historical epochs. The Bible demonstrates in human life how God becomes real—how He relates to the way we view ourselves, the way we relate to each other, our attitudes toward sex, our future, money-making, moral decisions. The Bible comes from heaven and gets down to earth. Like Jesus Himself it is fully human and fully divine at the same time.

A DIVINE BOOK

Since it is a divine book, we need to read it depending on the Holy Spirit who inspired its authors (2 Timothy 3:16). The promise is that the same Spirit who spoke through Paul lives in us, connecting us to God, opening our minds and making the Bible live as we read (1 Corinthians 2:9-16). We need, therefore, to read it *prayerfully.* "Lord, show me yourself as I read today. Call me, convict me, comfort me. I am open to you." We need to read it in *faith,* trusting God to work through His Word in us. We need to *meditate* upon it, allowing it to sink into us. Jesus says, *"If you abide in me, and my words abide in you, ask whatever you will, and it shall be done for you"* (1 John 15:7).

We need to allow the Bible to hit us as a total person: truth for our minds, feeling for our hearts, action for our wills. The question is not only what I believe and how I feel, but what I am going to do about it. Peter Marshall said, "People talk about problems in the Bible. My problems are with what I understand all too well." James put it this way, *"But be doers of the word, and not hearers only, deceiving yourselves"* (James 1:22 RSV).

While, then, the Bible is a divine book it is also a human book. After telling Timothy of its inspiration, Paul goes on to explain its purpose: it is *"profitable for teaching, for reproof, for correction, and for training in righteousness, that the man of God may be complete, equipped for every good work"* (2 Timothy 3:16-17 RSV). In other words, the Bible gives us content *(teaching),* conviction *(reproof),* new direction *(correction)* and the result is righteousness, completeness, fully doing the will of God.

A HUMAN BOOK

Since it is also a human book, we need methods or tools for study. This includes, first of all, a good modern translation. I recommend for serious study the *Revised Standard Version* or the *New American Standard Bible*. Paraphrases, such as *J. B. Phillips* or *The Living Bible* may be used for devotional reading.

Where should we begin? Start with the New Testament and read a Gospel, such as John, and one of the shorter letters, such as Philippians, at the same time— to learn who Christ is and how He applies to your practical Christian life.

A PERSONAL BOOK

As you read, ask some simple questions and write down your answers: Who? What? Where? When? Why? How? Who is speaking or acting? What is going on? Where does it happen? When is it? Why is it being done? How is it being done? You will not be able to apply all the questions to every passage, but use the ones that fit.

For example: John 3:16, *"For God so loved the world that he gave his only Son, that whoever believes in him should not perish but have eternal life."*

    Who?—God, His only Son, whoever

    What?—gave, not perish but have

    Where?—the world

    When?—have eternal life

    Why?—God so loved

    How?—whoever believes

Suddenly a simple verse takes life. All of the gospel is contained in a few words when we analyse them.

One other question is inescapable: *So what?* What am I going to do about it? The Bible is the living

24

word and God wants His Word to live in us. We must apply the Truth we learn.

We need to study the Bible for ourselves and we need to share the results of our study with each other. My brothers and sisters prevent me from becoming unbalanced in my Christian life as they share their comments and correctives with me. This means that I must have at least one other person who I study the Bible with—here is God's way of giving me encouragement and exhortation.

BY THE LIGHT FROM THE CROSS

A final word comes as a story. Some years ago in a mission church in Iran the lights went out during an evening service. The only illumination remaining came from a light behind the cross above the pulpit which was powered by a separate generator. The pastor who was reading the Scripture finished his reading by the light from the cross. That is the way we must read, by the light from the cross. Jesus Christ and Him crucified (1 Corinthians 2:2) is the clue to understanding all of Scripture. The written Word is to lead us to the living Word, Christ Himself, and to meet Him, rest in Him, be filled with Him is sufficient and satisfying. So study the Bible to know Christ and then make Him known in your world.

Conrad E. Lund | The Gifts of the Holy Spirit

Let me assure you, at the very beginning, that if you are a Christian, then you have received the Holy Spirit into your life. He is living in you. You cannot be a Christian apart from the Holy Spirit.

It was the Holy Spirit who convicted you of your sin, pointed you to Christ your Savior, and enabled you to say "yes" to the persistent call of God. It is the Holy Spirit, too, who daily shows us our dependence on our loving, benevolent heavenly Father. The language of Galatians 4:6 is unmistakably plain on this point. *"And because you are sons, God has sent the Spirit of His Son into our hearts, crying, 'Abba! Father!'"* RSV.

The Holy Spirit is not only the initial gift of God, the One who quickens in us the very life of Jesus Christ. He is also the giver of gifts by which we are enabled to participate in the sharing of his life.

26

THE CHARISMATIC AGE

It is our high privilege to live at a time of God's special visitation, a day when the Holy Spirit is giving His gifts to the church at large. Our Lord's corroboration of the message of Jesus Christ by His Spirit has caused our time to be called a *charismatic age,* that is, an age that abounds in manifestations of the Holy Spirit's gifts.

What are these manifestations? The catalog most often cited is that of 1 Corinthians 12:4-11.

NINE GIFTS

Nine gifts are mentioned in this summary. The nine gifts comprise three clusters of three. Three are power gifts, by which God expresses Himself through man. Three are revelation gifts, by which God discloses divine perceptions to man. Three are vocal or worship gifts, by which God speaks to and through man.

THE POWER GIFTS

These three constitute the power gifts: faith, the working of miracles, and gifts of healing.

Faith • The gift of faith is an invincible trust in God's power to do what He has commanded. Such faith dares to act in advance of God's provision of the proof. Elijah accepted and attested this gift of faith on Mt. Carmel (1 Kings 18:24ff). St. Paul bore witness by means of this "special faith" (1 Cor. 12:9, Weymouth) during a shipwreck (Acts 27). Every Christian as he "lives by faith, not by sight" (2 Cor. 5:7) is a candidate for this special endowment. Each of us, "according to the measure of faith which God has

27

assigned" (Rom. 12:3), should welcome he exercise of this gift.

Miracles • "The working of miracles" literally refers to "operations of works of power." A miracle is "a supernatural act on the natural plane."

The Apostle Peter pointed out the significance of such energy exhibited through the ministry of Jesus when he told of *"how God anointed Jesus of Nazareth with the Holy Spirit and with power; how He went about doing good and healing all that were oppressed by the devil, for God was with Him"* (Acts 10:38 RSV). It is the reality of God with his people that makes possible "the working of miracles," the acts that attest the power of God's hand upon His people (Eph. 2:10).

Healing • "Gifts of healing" refer to the employ-ment of the gift of faith and the gift of the working of miracles as ministering specifically to man's physical, emotional, and mental health. This particular manifes-tation of the Spirit was prominent in the ministry of Jesus from start to finish. The exercise of this gift can turn unbelieving hearts to God. Unbelief inhibits its exercise. It is for God Himself to decree where, when, and for whom this gift is to be the source of restora-tion to health. The three usual steps to its employment are: compassion for a given need; constraint to do something about it; and, finally, the conviction, born of the Spirit, that God will give the gift of healing through you. (See Acts 3:1-7 and 16.)

REVELATION GIFTS

The revelation gifts enable Christians to apply the heavenly Father's knowledge to the task of advancing His program. Two of them are tied to utterance. Wis-dom and knowledge God imparts to members of the family "for the common good," but they convey His intended benefit only when spoken out. The third revelation gift is "the ability to distinguish between spirits." To earnest followers of Jesus Christ whose very zeal may propel them into actions instigated by counterfeiting spirits, it is urgently necessary to receive this endowment. Even Satan's clever attempts to masquerade as an "angel of light" cannot succeed in the face of such God-given insight.

Wisdom • The utterance of wisdom is a disclosure of the purpose of God that gives "the assurance of things hoped for, the conviction of things not seen." By such a disclosure Noah built an ark for the salvation of his family, Joseph fled with Mary and Jesus to safety in Egypt, Peter overcame his reluctance to speak the words of life to non-Jewish hearers and James resolved an issue that threatened the division of the early church by saying, confidently, "It has seemed good to the Holy Spirit and to us." This is wisdom revealed by our heavenly Father.

Knowledge • The companion gift, the utterance of knowledge, is a divine disclosure of facts and information discoverable in no other way. By means of this gift Peter made the good confession on which Jesus builds the church. By means of the same gift he saw through an act of dishonesty that imperiled the Jerusalem church and interpreted the human events that caused some to question the delay of Christ's return. Scripture's own illustrations (Ananias about Saul, Acts 9:11; Jesus about the Samaritan woman, John 4:18, 19, 29, and about the hearts of men, John 2:24) make it clear beyond room for argument that neither natural nor acquired acumen is involved. This knowledge comes as a gift.

Discernment of Spirit • "The ability to distinguish between spirits" is the Lord's counter-intelligence program. When some "depart from the faith by giving heed to deceitful spirits and doctrines of demons," this insight will expose the deceit and set free those who will receive and love the truth. "Destructive heresies" and "the wicked deception" perpetrated by "the activity of Satan" threaten God's church today. The Spirit of God shares the corrective and enabling word by disclosing his discernment of enemy strategies and techniques.

WORSHIP (VOCAL) GIFTS

The worship (vocal) gifts of the Spirit enlarge the believer's delight in worshiping the Father in Spirit and in truth.

Three vocal, inspirational gifts are listed by St. Paul in the twelfth chapter of the first Corinthian letter: prophecy, various kinds of tongues, and the interpretation of tongues.

Prophecy • The gift of prophecy makes it possible to "speak for another." The emphasis is caught in the exhortation of 1 Peter 4:11, "whoever speaks, [let him speak] *as one who utters the oracles of God.*" It is the most important of the three worship or vocal gifts and therefore the one to "earnestly desire" (1 Cor. 14:1, see also v. 12).

By this gift, believers understand the gifts of God. St. Paul said, *"And we impart this in words not taught by human wisdom but taught by the Spirit."* The church is built up by the faithful acceptance and use of this gift. By prophecy the church can exhort, comfort, instruct, and convert.

30

Tongues • When believers spoke in other tongues, "as the Spirit gave them utterance" it was accepted as an evidence of the Holy Spirit's filling. By means of this endowment a believer can pray in the Spirit of God, can magnify God, can receive edification, and can experience an artesian well of assurance and satisfaction within his inner being. When used with the companion gift of interpretation, the gift of tongues is able to edify (build up, strengthen) the church.

This gift is the most controversial of the nine gifts listed in 1 Corinthians 12. The reason for this is anticipated in the third chapter. There Paul says, *"While there is jealousy and strife among you, are you not of the flesh, and behaving like ordinary men?"* (3:3 RSV). Strife may be instigated by those who are tongues-speakers when on the basis of this gift they draw wrong conclusions about their own spirituality or the inadequacies of fellow Christians who lack the gift. Then, again, "jealousy" infers the view of "have nots" who envy some "haves" and therefore seek reasons to impugn the gift.

The three-fold exhortation of Paul in Galatians 5:26 is of strategic importance for all who would "walk by" as well as "live by the Spirit." How welcome should be each gift of the Spirit by which God builds His church. All conceit, all provoking of one another ("challenging one another to rivalry," NEB) and all envy (being "ambitious for our own reputations" Phillips) needs to be resisted, tenaciously and perseveringly, by the positive endeavor to "outdo one another in showing honor." As we give place to the Word of God and in *"real warm affection for one another as between brothers (show a) willingness to let the other man have the credit"* (Romans 12:10, Phillips) we will deny to the devil a foothold for carrying out his scheme for division and destruction. We shall be less concerned about who has what gift and more unified in the common desire to uplift Jesus Christ as Savior and Lord.

Interpretation · The last of the nine gifts of the Spirit to be discussed in this article is that of "the interpretation of tongues." By means of this gift the Holy Spirit interprets to a group of believers the significance of a word delivered by means of the gift of tongues. It is interpretation, not translation, and hence may differ markedly in length from the word in tongues. Every tongue-speaker is encouraged to pray for the gift of interpretation.

TWO FINAL POINTS

A complete study of the gifts of the Spirit would consider also the lists of Romans 12:6-8 (cf. 9-13), Eph. 4:7-11 (cf. 12-16, noting the inclusive phrases that summon each believer to obedient response: *"by every joint," "when each part is working properly"*) and 1 Peter 4:10-11. What has been covered should be adequate, however, to emphasize two important points.

First, the Spirit of God is manifesting in our days the entire complement of those gifts by which God lives within and acts through his body, the church.

Second, the church needs to retain a single eye of devotion if the whole body is to be full of light. That single eye needs to fasten upon Jesus, *"the pioneer and perfecter of our faith."* In that view of Him we will correctly comprehend and manifest the gifts of the Spirit He pours out upon us.

Bob Turnbull

Will the Real Me Stand Up!

C'mon, what's wrong with me, anyway? This is ridiculous! I've got so much to be thankful for, yet I'm just wasting time, doing nothing, and going no place. What a waste!

I've got food in my stomach; I've got a roof over my head, clothes on my back, a free school to attend, parents who really care, a great country, good friends, a car to get around with, sports to participate in, some pretty girls to date, the whole scene. It's really neat. Yet, it isn't. Something is missing. Something just isn't right. But what? Whatever it is, it's bothering me.

WHAT ABOUT GOD?

I know what it is! Yeah, it's so obvious I've missed it. Here I am rattling on about material things and leaving out the most important part of my life. I guess I do that all the time. It's God—the Lord—the Holy Bible—prayers—heaven—and all that. I'm forgetting the most adventure-filled biblical promise in the sacred Scriptures, leastways for me, and that is Matthew 6:33, *"Seek first his kingdom and his righteousness, and all these things shall be yours as well"* RSV. Wow, and that promise is meant for all of us!

Here I am, a high school senior, getting ready for college and a career, and I continue to forget my Lord and Savior. Satan sure can influence my thoughts and get me side-tracked on other matters, away from really needed spiritual involvements with God. The real me keeps hesitating to stand up. That's probably because I don't know who the *real me* is. Ridiculous, isn't it? Here I am, a Christian by grace with a promised eternal life, forgiveness of all my sins and an exciting purpose to live each day. And I keep wallowing in matters that have no relevance to eternity, and to now, as a matter of fact. I guess I need to shout to myself, "Will the real me stand up!"

THE REAL ME, THE RENEWED ME

Like I say, I've got so much to be thankful for. It's time I really claim and apply Jesus' promises to my lifestyle, and let it be seen by all men and women. If the real me (the re-newed me) would stand up and be consistent in my standing up, wow, what an impact that would have on my friends, my teachers, my family, my community. They would no longer be seeing old-natured me, they would see new-natured me—a true Christian in every blessed sense of the word. Since I can't change myself, and won't even try, I'll just let the Holy Spirit go through me and do the house cleaning.

Let's see, where do we start?

FAMILY ME

I won't get uptight whenever anyone calls me "brother." Instead I'll be thankful that I'm recognized as part of God's forever family. A family that accepts the real me.

ETERNAL ME

I won't sweat death like I used to. Me, worried over dying. Silly, isn't it? I mean, here God promised me eternal life with Him, and I'm worrying about checking out of this nutty world. Worrying is wrong, too. If God is really in control, why worry about anything? We only worry because we take over and don't let God control our lives and our circumstances. I'm going to truly believe and be thankful for John 11:25 and 26, and have a happy forever.

CHOSEN ME

The real me is going to stand up and say, "I'm a chosen generation." Chosen by God, for God. 1 Peter 2:9 is talking to me when it speaks of being *"called out of darkness into his marvellous light."* The real me can be recognized when I stand in his light.

COMMITTED ME

When my "old" self was sitting on the premises instead of standing on the promises, I was uncommitted. And an uncommitted Christian is really gross. Now that the real born-again me is standing up, I can have a God-inspired, reckless daring with my total commitment. Yeah, that's right—total commitment. Anything less is just toothpaste. In 1 Timothy 4:12 we're told that we should *"set the believers an example in speech and conduct, in love, in faith, in purity."* That is commitment—pure and simple. Through God's grace now I know I can contribute to the needs of society with a positive program of helps. I'm not second-rate. I'm first-rate, because I'm the child of a first-rate God. I know I've been blessed with certain gifts, and the more I give them over to God, the more they are raised up—with His perfect timing. I've noticed my timing in the past leaves a bit to be desired, to say the least. Commitment without hesitation or reservation. Why didn't I think of that before?

Commitment also means that no one will tag me with being a "religious chicken." Yeah, I've dropped out before. Plenty of times. But there is no such animal in this Christian life. In Jeremiah 23:24 I'm told that there is no place to hide, so why have I tried to duck God in the past? Weird, aren't we? He's the "lover of my soul," not the "jailer of my soul." If I'm totally committed to God then I won't have any Satanical-induced dropout disease. Satan can't hassle me when I'm wearing that heavy Ephesians 6 armor.

OUTSPOKEN ME

Oh yes, I've got to commit to God the fact that from now on I am going to have to grab and hold on to my tongue. I don't mean literally hanging on to that slippery muscle in my mouth. I am talking about those times when I sometimes shift my tongue into high gear before I start my brain. This "talk now, think and repent later" syndrome, has got to go. I had better care what I say. God cares. I mean, when you read God's Word you come across 1 Corinthians

10:31, *"Whatever you do, do all to the glory of God."* That verse can sure be involved with our never-ceasing tongues. Petty gossip, cheap comments, slanderous innuendos, gross jokes, double-meaning statements, rumor spreading and all that garbage doesn't compute with God whose Son is called the Word. We should guard the statements we make.

THE REAL ME

Praise the Lord. The real me can stand up by God's grace and because of His patience. It's humbling, it's exciting, it's really happening to me because I've finally stopped trying and have started simply trusting. I've put down the "do-your-own-thing" cliché in both word and deed. I'm going to obey my parents, since God says so, and not hassle them. I'm going to stop putting everyone down, and start lifting them up. I'm going to look at others through the eyes of God's Word and see people as Jesus sees them. That's part of being the real me, seeing others as they really are.

"Thank you Lord, for saving my soul. Thank you, Lord, for making me whole." More than a song, it's a new life. When the real me, and you, stand up thing happen. All because of God's initial love.

Pardon me, I've got to go. I've got a lot of Christian living and loving to do!

Emotional Highs and Lows

William E. Berg

One day high. One day low. Yesterday you really loved Jesus. Today you wonder about Him. Some days He seems like a real Helper, but other days you think He forgot you. Your faith is strong one day, but the next you wonder if you believe at all. You're full of joy one day, but sunk in the valley of depression the next.

Does life have to be like that? If you believe Jesus is Savior and Lord, won't your faith make you happy all the time?

THE FLUCTUATION OF FEELINGS

(For Bible Study: Lamentations 3:1-26; Romans 7:21—8:2; Romans 8:18-39; Matthew 26:20-35; John 11:33-44; 1 Corinthians 15:55-58)

The Christian life is not a happiness cult or a healing cult. Nor is it an ecstatic cult. Jesus did not come to make us high or happy. He came to make us totally new persons in Himself. Someone has said, "I do not have enough religion to keep me from sinning, but just enough to take the joy out of it." Many a professing Christian would have to put it this way, "I have just enough religion to affect my emotions, but not enough to enlighten my mind and to control my will."

During a marriage service at the altar of a church the bridegroom was very nervous. His hands went in and out of his many pockets in a most distracting way. The best man whispered, "What happened, John? Did you lose the ring?" John moaned, "Worse than that. I've lost my enthusiasm."

Enthusiasm is not centered in the emotions. The word itself (coming from en theos) means "in God." The phrase "in Christ" or its equivalent is found 172 times in the New Testament. The central question is not, "How do you feel?" but rather, "In whom do you trust?"

Anna B. Mow, in her excellent book, *Going Steady with God,* gives this word picture of an emotional high and low following the sense of joy and peace when someone dedicates his or her life to God: "Too many people, however, look back to such an experience and remember only how they *felt.* Then later, when they are tired or sick or are using up all their spiritual energy meeting problems, and they don't *feel* as they did that first time, they foolishly think they have lost their experience. One girl said, 'I've been saved three times. I'm out again. What do I do now?' She really did not know what the score was. Your emotional status is not the thermometer for your spiritual health. From now on, no matter how you feel at any time, anywhere, God is there to stay with you—unless you put Him out."

The late Dr. E. Stanley Jones wrote, "I'm not on a mountaintop and I'm not in the valley. I'm on the Way." So don't go by your fluctuating feelings, but by the faith God offers you in an Unchanging Person.

THE UNWAVERING LOVE OF GOD

(For Bible Study: 1 Corinthians 13; Romans 5:1-11; John 3:16; 1 John 3:16; Luke 15:11-32)

When you feel defeated in your Christian life, besieged by doubts and confused by your feelings, remember the central fact of your faith—*God loves you.* Let us learn from the little girl whose mother in a devastating rebuke said, "Mother can't love you when you are bad." Later she found her little girl standing before a mirror sobbing and yet trying to sing, "Jesus loves me this I know, For the Bible tells me so." These were the words that Karl Barth, the famous theologian and scholar, said most adequately summed up his theological position! This central fact of God's love for bad people like us should put our feelings into place.

When you feel elated do not stand there singing and exulting. Get involved in a loving act. Enthusiasm is no substitute for obedience. Share someone's hurts. Bear the burden of another. Forget your own feelings long enough to empathize with others, seeking to know how they feel. And remember, *"We love because He first loved us"* (1 John 4:19 RSV).

If your feelings are pushing you up and down, remember the story of the young man in a mental health institution who pushed a wheelbarrow upside down all over the hospital grounds. When asked why he did not wheel it right side up, he replied, "Do you think I'm out of my mind? If I did that, they'd fill it!"

Let God fill you with His Holy Spirit as you open your life to Him in self-surrender. He will make you high on Jesus in mind, emotions and will. Jesus said in Luke 11:13, *"If you then, bad as you are, know how to give your children what is good for them, how much more will the heavenly Father give the Holy Spirit to them who ask him"* NEB.

How much more indeed! There is more for you than feelings. There is the fact of God's presence and power. So in my total being I shout, "Hallelujah!"

41

Ken Berven

How to Forgive Yourself and Others

Just before Jesus' death He was meeting with His disciples. They were sharing together in the upper room in the Last Supper. As the evening proceeded, Jesus told them what was going to happen to Him—that He would die on a cross (Matthew 26:2). Each of the disciples listened with concern.

Peter could not stand to think that Jesus would have to go through such an experience. He promised Jesus that he would be with Him to the bitter end, *"Even if I must die with You, I will not deny You"* (Matthew 26:35 RSV).

But Jesus knew they would not be able to keep their promises. He told Peter what was going to happen, *"Truly, I say to you, this very night, before the cock crows twice, you will deny me three times"* (Mark 14:30 RSV). He told Judas to do what he had to do quickly (John 13:27). Jesus knew His disciples better than they knew themselves.

Let's learn from these two disciples, Peter and Judas. They both had spent three years with Jesus as He poured His life into all the disciples. They had learned about God's love. They had learned about trusting Him from their experience. They knew Jesus had a special mission on this earth. They knew that He was the Messiah—the Savior of Israel. They both knew all of this, but in their sin and guilt they responded differently.

COME TO JESUS—GUILT AND ALL

Peter the rock became Peter the sand. He sank into his guilt trip and could only reason, "Jesus is dead. No one ever came back from death. How could I have ever hoped that Jesus would establish a new kingdom here on earth?" But Jesus did return and appear to Peter and the disciples on two occasions. Still Peter was plagued by his denial. His guilt remained and he found it hard to forgive himself.

One night following a frustrating but unsuccessful night of fishing Jesus appeared again to His disciples (John 21:1-19). Peter talked to Jesus alone that night and got his guilt squared away.

Jesus knew of Peter's guilt and wanted to see if that guilt would hinder his love. Three times Jesus asked if Peter still loved Him (John 21:15-17). And three times Jesus showed His love and acceptance to Peter through a forgiving call to service. Knowing that he was forgiven changed the course of Peter's life. And later in his letters to believers Peter makes a strong point of reminding them that they are forgiven (2 Peter 1:9-12).

With Judas it was different. Judas did not know how

to handle his guilt problem. This whole matter had gotten out of hand. Jesus was crucified all because of his sin. Even trying to return the blood money didn't work out. "How can I ever forgive myself of this mess," he reasoned. These and other thoughts flooded Judas' head as he left the sanctuary. Even though Judas had heard the same message as Peter, he could not reconcile himself to his misdeed and forgive himself. To live with this guilt was too much. The result was he went out and hanged himself. Unreconciled failure and unforgiven guilt drove Judas to suicide.

As Peter learned to live in his forgiveness he went on to lead the disciples and together they turned the world rightside up. Peter knew his faults and errors, but accepted them and His forgiveness. Yet Judas is an example of so many of us today who have heard the message of the gospel but have never been able to forgive ourselves when we do wrong. Many have gone the same route as Judas because their guilt trip was too heavy.

JESUS, THE SOURCE OF OUR FORGIVENESS

Whenever we consider this subject of forgiveness, we must always remember that Jesus Christ had more to forgive others for than anyone else who ever lived. Jesus took the rap for everyone. When Christ bore the sins of all men to the cross and shed His blood in payment, He suffered in His physical death the pain and anguish no one had ever experienced. But the physical pain was nothing compared to the spiritual anguish of having God forsake Him because of our sins.

How did Jesus deal with others who wronged Him?

In the case of His parents who rebuked Him for not returning to Nazareth with them, He merely said, *"Did you not know that I must be in my Father's house?"* (Luke 2:49 RSV). He did not seem up-tight, just confident of Himself and where He was going. He lived in subjection to His parents but lovingly let them know why He stayed in Jerusalem.

Many times Christ's ministry came into conflict with the religious leaders. They were always putting Him down because He made religious life too simple. Jesus never struck out at them critically but loved them and accepted them. Jesus' statement from the cross is His prime example of forgiveness. As He was suffering and dying after being falsely accused, He interceded with His Father on behalf of His killers. While in pain on the cross He said, *"Father, forgive them; for they know not what they do"* (Luke 23:34 RSV). Even in death Jesus knew how to forgive.

FORGIVENESS MEANS ACCEPTANCE

On a human level, to forgive others is to be able to accept others. As we look at the faults of other people, we accept them because we see ourselves in them. We too have the capacity to irritate and hurt others. On the same basis, to forgive ourselves is to be able to accept ourselves as we are. In that acceptance we are following Jesus' command to love ourselves. Loving ourselves does not mean that we condone our evil actions. It does mean that we know and accept ourselves as we are. Then we can forgive ourselves of the sin and inconsistencies in our Christian lives. When Peter knew that in himself he was not the rock, he could forgive himself for denying Jesus.

How can this practically apply to us today? How can we learn to live in forgiveness of ourselves and others? We will never be able to forgive others until we have learned to love and accept ourselves. The key is to see and accept ourselves and others the way that God does. God loves and accepts us not on the basis of what we have done, but on what Jesus Christ has done on our behalf.

God has declared you forgiven eternally. *"For by a single offering He has perfected for all time those who are sanctified"* (Hebrews 10:14 RSV). God declares you perfect and forgiven, past, present, future. This He can do only because He has been satisfied for all your sin. It is the blood of Jesus that is today before the Father cleansing you of all your sin. The issue with God, therefore, is not your sins. The issue is whether or not you believe in Jesus as your personal Savior. As we see ourselves as forgiven we can begin to see others that way too. We can forgive others. *"Be kind to one another, tenderhearted, forgiving one another, as God in Christ forgave you"* (Ephesians 4:32 RSV).

In Hebrews 2:11 we see that Jesus who sanctifies and we who are sanctified are one. Jesus looks on us and sees us as being one with Him. He sees us as He sees Himself. Jesus is not ashamed to call us His brethren. Therefore, since He forgave others, we too can forgive those who hurt us. Jesus basically is saying, "Since I forgave you, you too can forgive others."

How to Handle Temptation

Robert M. Overgaard

We are all troubled by temptations. And the trouble that temptations bring is not just annoyance but defeat. We are tempted, we give in, we are defeated, we give up. It's difficult to be "more than conquerors" when we can only cling to survival by our fingernails. Temptation overtakes us all.

So how can we handle temptation?

FIRST AID

First, the first aid treatment: **run.** Escape is often a simple matter of geography: from where you are being tempted to somewhere out of reach. If necessary, leave your coat (Genesis 39:7-13). If you don't want to be stung, stay away from the bees.

Running won't solve the problem for long, so you must take the next step: **pray.** Invite God to come to your rescue. If we really invite the Lord into our tempting situation, the entire atmosphere will change. We will see the whole scene in new perspective. God is able to deliver all who call upon Him (Hebrews 2:18, 1 Corinthians 10:13).

God is always able to deliver us from temptation, but often we do not want to be delivered. We do not run away, we do not pray. This points up the limitations of a first aid approach. The situation which invites us to do evil is not the only problem. We, ourselves, are part of the problem if we are ill-prepared to meet the tempting situation.

PREVENTIVE AID

Missionary doctors tell us that preventive medicine isn't very glamorous. Most people would rather have a shot of a miracle drug than dig wells, improve sanitation, and change health habits. Yet, preventive medicine can help thousands avoid sicknesses, while drugs may be available only to a few.

Our repeated learning of the Ten Commandments may have seemed tedious, but if we were blessed with this preventive aid, alarm bells ring through our whole system when we are tempted to break one of these great laws of mental and spiritual health.

But many temptations are subtle, and we don't see the full danger at first. That we are about to break a commandment may not be obvious. For this reason we need the preventive aid of clear Biblical thinking. David said, *"I have laid up thy word in my heart, that I might not sin against thee"* (Psalm 119:11 RSV). A mind well taught in the Word, in the setting of Christian sharing, can give us a right understanding of a tempting situation. Pray for understanding, the Lord will give you wisdom so you will be prepared (James 1:5). Preventive aid helps.

"Helps, yes, but sometimes it isn't enough help. Sometimes I sin anyway."

CORRECTIVE AID

Some sin problems require corrective aid. The correction may have to be more profound than radical surgery.

A man with a sensitive stomach and a tension-producing job spent years living on antiacid pills and milk. After his eleventh ulcer he decided to do something about it. He had his whole stomach removed. While recovering he started to reevaluate his lifestyle. With the new freedom from pain came a new strength to face up to the task of reorganizing his life. He was like a new man through corrective surgery.

Does God have a radical surgery plan for defeated Christians? Yes, He does. His corrective aid brings us right to the cross. Most of us shy away from the cross. We would rather have aspirin or warm milk.

We may not be ready for the cross until we know how bad our condition is. We may be bleeding to death through ulcers while avoiding a crucifixion. We may be in bad shape and only dimly realize it.

Paul tells us how surprised he was to discover what sin he really had in his own heart. *"For I do not do the good I want, but the evil I do not want is what I do"* (Romans 7:19 RSV).

Sound familiar? You may have some sin problems which are so profound, that the only thing to do is to face up to the fact that you are helpless. Quit struggling. Try until you die, then die! (Romans 7:11, 14).

What then? If you move over, God will have a chance.

God wants to lead us, when it is necessary, to the bitter end. He wants to show us the power of sin, the sinfulness of sin, the hateful nature of sin until like Paul we cry out, *"Wretched man that I am! Who will deliver me from this body of death."* He answers with the realization that deliverance will have to come from outside himself: *"Thanks be to God through Jesus Christ our Lord!"* (Romans 7:25). Here is the radical corrective of death to all our own powers.

REDEMPTIVE AID

If corrective aid is necessary, there must be something to fill this vacuum of death! There is.

Doctors can't heal anyone; they can only aid healing. The healing forces are already in the body through creation. When God heals us from sin, He is working with great creative power to make all things new. Through Jesus Christ He offers both initial and continuous redemptive aid. He heals us by bringing us into a conscious, living relationship with Himself as He credits our sin to the Lord's account and embraces us with His love.

When we know our sin, with the knowledge born in a broken and contrite heart, we are open to the healing love based on God's just solution to our dilemma. In the midst of our despair He surprises us again, this time with healing words, *"There is therefore now no condemnation for those who are in Christ Jesus"* (Romans 8:1 RSV).

What does this have to do with helping us to overcome temptation? It takes the monkey off our back!

You don't have to be successful in overcoming temptation to be right with God. You do need to repent and believe, but you don't have to perform. You are a child, loved of God, even if you are a weak child. Since this is true, you can relax and take time to let God make all things new. The foundation is the knowledge that there is no condemnation to those who are trusting in Christ. Our faith is in a historical cross where Christ established the basis for a new life. The more consciously we build our lives on this foundation, the more likely we are to be open to His Spirit and power.

NUTRITIONAL AID

If redemptive aid creates a new basis for freedom from the sinful life, the positive daily antidote to temptation is nutritional aid.

"You are what you eat," a modern dietician has written. *"Walk by the Spirit, and do not gratify the desires of the flesh,"* Paul says in Galatians 5:16. We are accepted as we trust Christ. Now as sons we set new goals. We mind the things of the Spirit (Romans 8:5).

In the deepest sense, we can best avoid temptation by becoming spiritual men! Let's overcome temptation by giving, yielding our lives in a new relationship to God that by His Spirit we may be filled with love, joy, peace, patience, kindness, goodness, faithfulness, gentleness, self-control (Galatians 5:22).

Try nutritional aid! Here is a life worth living. Why give way to sin when life can be found only in right relationships?

It all starts and ends with Jesus. *"He who believes in the Son has eternal life"* (John 3:36).

Sex and the Single Christian

Pete Gillquist

Without question, the number one problem facing the high school and college student today is the temptations which accompany sex. At the present time the problem of drugs is getting more attention in the news media and from the public. But even drugs are often a means of "getting it on" with sexual activity.

And there's no doubt about it—sexual expression between a man and a woman, whether the full act of intercourse or just the preliminaries, is fantastically enjoyable. God meant it to be.

In this article I want to (1) show God's purpose in giving us the gift of sex, (2) relate sex to the biblical understanding of marriage and (3) look at what Scripture says about people who have 'messed up' in their sexual experiences.

THE MEANING OF SEX

I've talked with a lot of kids who have lived their lives with the morals of an alley cat. They say, "Sex doesn't mean anything to me anymore. I've slept around so much I'm almost numb. In fact, sex is repulsive to me."

Did you know that it is natural for a permissive person to feel that way? Why? Because they have taken something that God has given and missed the whole point of why God gave it to us. But before we can understand the gift of sex, we must first understand the purpose of a much bigger item—marriage.

THE PURPOSE OF MARRIAGE

The reason marriage is such a big deal is because it is a picture or representation of something else. Marriage is an earthly illustration of the relationship between Jesus Christ and the people who belong to Him. God says, *"For the husband is the head of the wife as Christ is the head of the church"* (Ephesians 5:23 RSV).

Scripture says that our marriages are intended to mirror on earth God's love and commitment to us in Jesus Christ. That's one reason why our marriages are intended to last forever—"till death do us part." God never divorces Himself from his commitment to us. Therefore, since we are to mirror God's fidelity, our husband/wife unity is designed to be permanent too.

THE RELATIONSHIP OF SEX TO MARRIAGE

Now, here's the matter that comes as a surprise to many. If marriage, a joining together of a man and woman, is a picture of the joining together of Jesus and his people, what is it that gets a marriage started? What is the event that begins a marriage?

"That's easy," you say, "isn't it a wedding, a ceremony?" No! It's not a ceremony. Merely going through a wedding ceremony will not make you married, just like saying a ceremonial formula will not make you a Christian.

The event that God has chosen to symbolize the beginning of marriage is sexual intercourse. That's why the Apostle Paul says, *"He who joins himself* (has intercourse with) *to a prostitute becomes one body with her? For, as it is written, 'The two shall become one' "* (1 Corinthians 6:16 RSV). Did you see it? A man and a woman become one by the act of sexual intercourse. Wow! That sure elevates the sex act. What I am saying is that God places far more importance on sex than most people do.

So when God says, "Cool it on your sex life outside of marriage," He does so for a very important reason. God doesn't want you to become "one flesh" with somebody other than the one who will be your mate for life. God is watching out for your best interest! And, since Jesus Christ lives in us, He is part of us.

The Apostle Paul says that our body is a "temple" where God lives, *"Do you not know that your body is a temple of the Holy Spirit within you, which you have from God? You are not your own; you were bought with a price. So glorify God in your body"* (1 Corinthians 6:19-20 RSV). What a slap in the Lord's face it is for his children to involve him in open sin, by engaging in intercourse on a "one-nighter" basis. That's just plain cheap!

WHAT IF YOU HAVE ALREADY BLOWN IT?

God says there is complete forgiveness and restoration for *anyone* who comes to him. *"I will remember their sins and their misdeeds no more"* (Hebrews 10:17

RSV). But let's take a moment and consider what our sins are as we look at their remedy.

1. *Intercourse outside of marriage* is obviously a sin. The word used in Scripture to describe this is "fornication," which means two unmarried people committing the sex act. The Bible calls married people who engage in sex outside of their marriage "adulterers." And both "fornication" and "adultery" are called sin. *"Do you not know that the unrighteous shall not inherit the kingdom of God? Do not be deceived; neither fornicators, nor idolaters, nor adulterers . . . shall inherit the kingdom of God"* (1 Corinthians 6:9-10, NASB).

2. *Sexual caressing* is a "turn-on" for the flesh which leads to further involvement. Let's face it. The purpose of petting is to gear each other up for sexual intercourse. We try to explain our way around that fact, but we can't. Now I'm not talking about holding hands, putting your arm around a girl friend or boy friend, kissing, or other signs of care and affection. What I am referring to is the caressing of the sex organs, whether over clothing or under clothing. Paul said, *"It is well for a man not to touch a woman"* (1 Corinthians 7:1). Petting is not an end in itself; it is the means to an end, namely intercourse. Thus, God has designed this expression of love uniquely for marriage.

3. *The gay scene* is an aberration of God's plan. *"Neither effeminate, nor homosexuals . . . shall inherit the kingdom of God* (1 Corinthians 6:9-10, NASB). That does not mean God hates "gay" folks. He doesn't, He loves them, but He hates their sin. It also means that homosexuality and lesbianism are not God's patterns for people's lives. God says that what they are into is sin.

55

GOD'S SOLUTION

What is God's solution? The Bible says, *"Walk by the Spirit, and do not gratify the desires of the flesh"* (Galatians 5:16). This command is for all of us, regardless of our backgrounds and specific sins. God says that if we simply allow our lives to be controlled by him, that we will be re-made in his image. We will not have to go on experiencing the results of alienation from him.

Speaking to the issue of your past sexual sin, God says, "Bag it. Turn from it. Phase it out." Speaking to the issue of your future life, God says, "Let Christ be your everything, your reality."

Tell Jesus Christ that you don't even have the will or the power to stop sinning against your body. Then ask Him to completely remake you so that the Holy Spirit living within you will make you different. It's possible. It's His promise to you. Take Him at His word.

Through the blood of Jesus you are clean, regardless of what you have done. Let Him be your Lord. Let Him take the control center of your life. Ask Christ to be your life, and give you a fresh, new start—beginning right now.

Additional Help from the Scriptures

1. Proverbs 6:20—7:27
2. Ephesians 5:22-33
3. 1 Corinthians 6:12—7:7

Further Reading and Study

"Love, Sex and Marriage," a cassette tape by Pete Gillquist, available through Lutheran Youth Alive, P.O. Box 2375, Van Nuys, California 91404.

"Sex and the Single Christian," a cassette tape by Pete Gillquist available through Lutheran Youth Alive, P.O. Box 2375, Van Nuys, California 91404.

The Christian Family, by Larry Christenson, published by Bethany Fellowship, Minneapolis, Minnesota.

Booze, Grass, and Hard Stuff

Allan and Eunice Hansen

We are writing to you from what some have called a drug rehabilitation center. In the space of two years we have shared our family life with 25-30 youth at any one time. Over 600 young people lived with us. Listen to the stories of the kids who have shared life with us. Learn with us what we have seen God doing.

There are some who think we should try to scare youth from becoming involved in drugs. We have found that this is the wrong approach. The scare technique might even do more to increase the use of drugs than to decrease it. Youth are seeking for adventure, dangerous adventure, which drugs provide. Some are so fed up with life that it really does not matter whether they live or die. They are not afraid to die, so why try to scare them with the threat of death?

Life has been hard, frustrating, and disappointing for many of those using drugs and alcohol. They want to escape that life, to have some kicks, to find a life with happiness.

But the drug route brings unhappiness. Look at these comments made from the youth in our home who have been on the drug and drink route: "In the last three months, I had overdosed three times, slashed my wrists once. Those months were nothing but hell." "I had been taking drugs for 14 years, eight of those years on heroin. I spent four years in jail. I felt so alone it wasn't even funny." "Today, I have no desire to return to the mess." "I'm 27 years old, drink was my problem, I lost my wife. It was all such a bummer." If any happiness can come from the drug scene, then we have been talking to the wrong people.

DRUGS ARE JUST A SYMPTOM

Most Christian drug rehabilitation centers do not spend much time on drug information programs. This is because drug use is not the fundamental problem to be solved. Drug use is a symptom of deeper, under-lying problem. And our attention should be placed on the problem rather than on the symptom.

The fundamental problem is spiritual. We are born out-of-tune with God. Our sin has separated us from God who loves us. We are out of fellowship with Him. To put it bluntly, our lives are messed up. And as our messed-up lives are straightened out, the need for drugs will naturally disappear.

This all happens when Christ comes into our life and takes control. The spirit of Christ dwells in us, so we love the things God loves and hates the things he hates. We now have his new nature as well as our old nature.

One girl told us about the first time she went home following Christ's work in her life. Before she met

Christ, she told her friends to have a big party planned when she came home. But, when she got home, she did not want any drug parties. For now she was a new creature. The spirit of Christ was within her. Jesus Christ had given to her His abundant life. She no longer needed to search for it in things and places where it could not be found. She had been given the love and joy of life through the work of the Holy Spirit; the necessity to escape into an unreal world was gone. *"Therefore if any man is in Christ, he is a new creature; the old things passed away; behold, new things have come"* (2 Corinthians 5:17 NASB).

PASSING THE BUCK

One of the things we usually do is put the blame for our failures on someone else—we pass the buck. But if we want to deal honestly with our past failures, we must first admit that we did wrong *because we wanted to.* We must come to realize our own responsibility for the trips we are on, whether it's the so called insanity trip, drug trip, drink trip, rebellion trip, immorality trip, or the homosexuality trip. We must acknowledge our responsibility and want a change to take place.

FORGIVENESS SETS US FREE

When we realize that we are responsible for our messed up lives, then we'll know we can't help ourselves. We need God's mercy and forgiveness if we want to be "new creatures." The Bible says that we deserve to die because of the lives we live, but Christ takes our penalty and offers us forgiveness. The condition for receiving this is simple repentance, which means to turn from sin and turn to God, accepting His forgiveness through Christ.

Christ said, *"If the Son makes you free, you will be free indeed"* (John 8:36 RSV). We can now say *no* to our sin and *yes* to His righteousness. This is the first step of a new life: we must recognize Jesus Christ as our Lord and Savior.

SPEAK THE TRUTH

The second step is for you to state what you are in Christ: *"I am forgiven"* (I John 1:9). *"I am holy"* (Romans 11:16). *"I am pure"* (Isaiah 53:5). *"I am a child of God"* (John 1:12). *"I am the light of the world"* (Matthew 5:4). *"I am the salt of the earth"* (Matthew 5:3). *"I am a new person, the new creature in Jesus"* (2 Corinthians 5:17). *"My body is a temple of the Holy Spirit"* (1 Corinthians 6:19). Go ahead, say it out loud. Shout it! We are encouraged by verbalizing these scriptural truths. It is easy but wrong for us to say, "I am a poor, weak sinner," when we have been forgiven, when we have the very power within that raised Christ from the dead. We must state what we are.

PSALMS FOR ALL SEASONS

The third step is to be learned from the Psalms. God is concerned about our attitudes. We should give thanks to God (Psalm 95); rejoice (Psalm 100) and sing (Psalm 96:1). Singing has always been a mark of joy. Because of Christ's redemptive life, because of His love, because of His forgiveness, Christians sing. Giving thanks, rejoicing, and singing are not optional, they are commands from God. And they are part of Christ's transformation program in which He transforms us to be like himself.

EXPECT MIRACLES

As part of God's forgiven, delivered family, we should expect miracles of leading and guidance. As an undeserved blessing of God, we should expect to meet the right people, at the right time, and at the right place (Luke 2:27; Acts 10). God is now living in us, he's in control of our life. Therefore, we should expect the supernatural events as well as the natural.

STUDY THE BIBLE

In the Bible we find out how Jesus wants us to live and what He wants us to do. But this means that we must get into the Word. And when we do, we will discover that God not only has forgiven us, He wants us to forgive others. He wants us to forgive and make reconciliation with parents (Matthew 14:15), be obedient to parents (Ephesians 6:1), live holy lives (1 Peter 2:11), be generous (John 3:17), help others, (James 1:27), serve others (1 John 3:16), be all-out for Christ (John 15:8), and be in Christian fellowship. All this we discover from the study of God's word, the Bible.

Simple? Yes, but these steps are creating miracles. Minds are being restored, bodies are being healed, relationships are being renewed. People need to be made new, and there is only one way—through Jesus Christ.

Have you gone the drug route? Is your life controlled by booze, grass, or hard stuff? Then know this—God wants you to be whole, not broken. God loves you, forgives you, restores you, and makes you holy. Just trust in Him and be His new creature.

61

My New Brothers and Sisters

Charles S. Mueller

The day you decided to be a vital, involved, essential part of the Christian community was the day you made one of the best decisions of your life. Led by God's Spirit you took a great step. Did you join the church for the first time? Or was it more of a determination to finally, *really* join the church? Either decision is O.K. It puts you right in the middle of one of life's most exciting adventures.

I suppose, even now, you must be still sorting out some of your feelings, or facing a few not-so-appealing realities. By now you should be more fully sensing what "joining a church" means. What thoughts are spinning through your mind?

> I'm so happy about what I've done. It makes me feel good all day long. But, wait a minute. What will my friends think? Do all of them know? Will they want to be around me any more?

Is that what you are thinking? Well, maybe your

friends-of-before won't want to be around you any more. It's possible. It depends on what kind of friends you had, and the experiences you and your friends shared. There's no doubt that you are a matter of concern for them. Your decision to be an active Christian has to have an effect upon them. If they haven't been following the will of God, your new style of life is going to clash with their standards. You can't mix oil and water. Or, to put it another way, you can't mix *flesh* and *spirit* (Galatians 5:16-25). I suspect that some of your old friends aren't going to be as friendly any more. You no longer have as much in common with them. So how can you maintain the same level of relationship?

But don't worry. God always puts something better in the place of those things which, for His sake, we lay aside. Have you sensed that already? Perhaps you've thought:

> There's no use getting disturbed by what my old friends may feel. I certainly don't want to hurt them. If they leave me, they leave me. I know I have a new and wonderful friend in Christ.

Real friendship is beautiful. And now, in Jesus Christ, you have a new and better friend than ever before. He is the greatest friend the world has ever seen. Not only will He sacrifice for and love those who are His friends (John 15:13), but He will do as much for those who are His enemies (Romans 5:8). We know He will do that, because He did that! Jesus Christ died for us that we might live. And that life isn't something that is going to begin only in the future, it is something that begins right now. Through your friendship with Christ you will daily experience the abundant life in the fellowship of all the other members of God's family. Have you gotten that far in your thinking?

> That's right, I almost forgot! I not only have a Friend—I have friends! That's what the church is all about. I've become part of a family, with brothers and sisters, and mothers and fathers, and all those other wonderful relationships that make a family!

Right again! You do have a new and wonderful family. Some churches still have the lovely custom of speaking to one another as "brother" and "sister." There's nothing wrong with that! It's very biblical. This great practice reflects the idea of the fellowship (and family) of faith.

God looks on us as His family. If you doubt that, read John 1:12, or Romans 8:14, or 1 John 3:1, or Romans 9:26. I should say we are a family! Our Brother, Jesus, took us by hand to His Father in heaven. His Father adopted us (Galatians 4:4-6)! And now we are a functioning part of the family. As adopted sons of God we are joint heirs with Christ of the Kingdom of God (Romans 8:17; James 2:5). And that's really part of God's forever family.

> Family! Really family! I do have something better than what I had! Once I only had friends. Now I have friends who are real brothers and sisters.

The church, God's "called-out" family, is more than a gathering of strangers who accidently happen to be in the same place at the same time. Our relationship to each other is stronger than that. We are blood relatives. There courses through our veins the blood of our ancestral parents, Adam and Eve. And of course that is a bond which all humanity shares. But we are

64

more than that. We are united in the blood of Jesus Christ, God's Son, which cleanses us from all sin (1 John 1:17). In the church we are blood relatives—twice over!

> Part of a family. That's great. I want God to help me really be a part of this family—not just someone who lives under the same roof, but a member who knows what it means to be a family and is eager to put this knowledge to practice.

I hope those are your thoughts. There's so much that could be said about being in Christ's family. We do have family standards. Sadly enough, not everyone in the family always lives up to those family standards. Sometimes, just like in the "other" life, a brother or sister slips, and forgets. What do we do then? We go get them, seek them out, help them up, bring them back home. That's part of family living too.

Maybe, about right now, your mind is still drifting back to those "old" friends. That's O.K. God wants them too. You are very special to Him, but so are they. He wants them to become part of His family too. He has already made it possible if they'll just come home. Ask God to use you in bringing your old friends into this new family you've found.

New brothers and sisters in Christ. Look around you. We're all over the world. You have so much in common with us—and we with you. A common faith, a common experience, and a common claim on an uncommon Christ. He made us all a family. He gave us to each other as brothers and sisters. Let's rejoice in it! Be a part of it. Love it. And by the power of the Holy Spirit, let's expand it. There's always room for more in God's family.

Don Fladland

Getting It
Together
with
My Family

The stillness and quiet of the night was shattered by the ring of my telephone. A frantic young voice said, "Sue has tried to take her own life." Sue hated her home—everything and everyone in it. Her home was one constant hassle. There were fights about everything—money, friends, clothes, hair, school, dates, and comparisons of brothers and sisters. You name it, they fought over it.

In her heart welled up a deep ache of loneliness and frustration, and Sue, 14 years old, tried to take her own life.

During my years of working with youth and their families I have heard hundreds of these stories of broken family relationships. Selfishness, brutality, unfaithfulness, drunkenness, lack of communication and love have often resulted in bitterness and separation. How can we do battle against self-pity and bitterness? How can a lonely and embittered youth know love when all his life the opposite has been demonstrated to him? How can a frantic housewife cope with the task of keeping the family together when her husband is an alcoholic? How can children face the ugly fact that their parents can't stand them at home because "they get in the way"?

Recently I visited a Junior High School in a large metropolitan city where 52% of the youth came from broken homes. These homes have known the shattering heartbreak of divorce, runaway children, runaway parents, sickness, traumatic shock, financial pressures, sex hangups, and deep personality conflicts. Into this setting of frustration, tension, and conflict, God speaks through His love letter, the Bible. And He promises us and our families that through His Son Jesus Christ we can "get it together."

GOD CARES FOR YOU

God didn't just talk about His love and concern for our families, He demonstrated it by sending Jesus Christ to bring us together as an intimate part of His forever family. *"For God loved the world so much that He gave His only Son so that anyone who believes in Him shall not perish but have eternal life"* (John 3:16, LB.) The power and truth of this biblical principle has transformed broken homes and lives and given them a fresh beginning. *"Let Him have all your worries and cares, for He is always thinking about you and watching everything that concerns you"* (1 Peter 5:7 LB). God not only cares for us individually but for our entire family. The aim of Satan is to disrupt and destroy the family. God's purpose is to preserve and keep the family together.

GOD FORGIVES YOU

At the heart of this message is the beautiful possibility of new and deep relationships. All this is based on forgiveness. Getting it together is only possible because of God's grace and forgiveness for each member of the family. *"You [husband and wife] are joint heirs of the grace of life"* (1 Peter 3:7 RSV). Just as God loves us, forgives us, and removes our sin so we also can be given the power to forgive those who hurt us and sin against us. God's forgiveness is beautifully spelled out in the words of the Psalmist. *"He has removed our sins as far away from us as the east is from the west" (Psalm 103:12 LB).* David understood what it was like to go through life trying to cover his sins. No release came for him until he called up the Lord and accepted His forgiveness.

GOD LOVES YOU

Many search and struggle to find the key to happiness. However, when love is rejected and a person is shut out, bitterness and an unforgiving attitude will often result. The world of hurt is felt deeply by all members of a family. The beautiful part about Christ's love is that it goes right to the source of hurt.

The impact of what Christ can do to bring a family together is beautifully brought out in the experience of a college student. Candy was lonely and estranged from her family. She was a petite, brown-eyed brunette with a sweet shyness about her. Within this girl was a deep unrest and an aching heart. She was introduced to the Good News of Jesus Christ. She discovered that Christ could make her a new person and give her a fresh start. The frustrations of her childhood

68

and youth had never been resolved and now through faith she received Christ into her life. *"But to all who received Him, He gave the right to become children of God. All they needed to do was to trust Him to save them" (John 1:12 LB).* Immediately Candy was flooded with an overwhelming desire to fly home and tell her father something she had never told him before. Upon her arrival home she ran up to her father and said with tears flooding her eyes, "Daddy, I love you," and they embraced.

The contrast of the two illustrations used is striking. The girl I mentioned at the beginning of this article tried to resolve her family conflicts and frustrations through self-indulgence and self-destruction. The other girl chose to bridge the gap of family conflict and hassles through surrender to Christ's all-embracing love. "Getting it together" with any family is possible through the greatest force in the world today, God's love as revealed in Jesus Christ. Let's "get it together" God's way.

Dave
Anderson

How
Can I
Plug into
My Church?

What comes to your mind when you think of the word *church*? How's this for beginners? Ladies aid, church council, committees, ushers, acolytes, altar guild, choir, annual meeting, budget, building fund, music, and last but not least—Youth Sunday. Are these your thoughts when the word *church* is spoken? We might call this the "do" picture of the church. These are some of the activities the church does and some of the people that do them.

Now there is a "be" side of the picture also. And perhaps your thoughts are found in this list: the body of Christ; loving, caring, learning, growing, accepting, praying, gifted fellowship; chosen race; family of God; royal priesthood; household of faith. This is what the church is. And when we combine the "do" list and the "be" list, that's a lot of plug into.

We should clarify one important point. How can we plug into something which we already are? We are the church; anyone who is a Christ is a member of the "holy Christian Church, the community of saints," the "family of God," the "body of believers."

If you are a Christian, you are already plugged into the church. Jesus Christ has plugged you into His body. Christ has already taken the initiative. When He called us to Himself, He called us to one another. Therefore, if you know Christ as Savior you are already plugged into His church, His body.*

And the "Body of Christ" is made visible on earth through that divine/human organization called First Lutheran Church, Zion Baptist Church, All Saints Episcopal Church, Pentecostal Holiness Church, St. Mary's Catholic Church, Calvary Chapel. There are many different names to this institution of God. Look through the listings under "churches" in the yellow pages of your telephone book. You are a member of one of them. And how can you plug into it? That is the question.

THAT'S A FINE ATTITUDE TO HAVE

Let's talk about attitude. The attitude of many is negative. "My church is dead." "My church isn't spiritual (or spirit-filled)." "No one cares about youth." "My church will never change. They have to do things the way they've always done them or not at all." Some of us need to have our negative attitudes turned around before we can plug in.

I know a girl who thought she was the only Christian in her entire church. Then one summer she trav-

---

Reader, if you are not a personal Christian, if you do not know Jesus Christ as your Savior, then read the article on "The Way of Salvation" by Oswald Hoffmann. Accept by faith what Christ has done for you. Let Christ plug you into His church, right now.

eled with a team of witnessing youth. They visited five different congregations spending two weeks in each congregation. Her negative attitudes began to change as she visited these other churches. Wherever she went she saw signs of problems and signs of life. And she saw God alive and active wherever she went.

At the end of the summer my friend returned home. She had a new attitude toward herself, her family, and her church. She discovered that her home congregation was not so "out of it" after all. Her pastor told me, "Elaine came to me soon after she returned home asking how she could help. Our long conversation closed with a prayer—at her suggestion. During the next several months I saw her positive witness catch fire. Soon our youth began gathering for Bible study and service projects. Several adults became more involved in the life and mission of our church. I began to realize a new attitude toward my own ministry. Now she's away at college but the effects of her positive attitude and witness live on." So said her pastor!

A positive attitude—it's contagious!

COMMITMENT

Despite the lowering of the voting age, statistics show that youth are not exactly flocking to vote at the polls. Why? Perhaps our commitment is not deep enough. The same is true of our commitment to the church.

I have had to ask myself: Am I committed to the fellowship of believers to which I belong? Committed to the people in that fellowship? Committed to the pastor of the fellowship? When I am committed to them, I care about them. I'm concerned about what goes on. I'm concerned enough about my pastor and who he is that I'll go to him and tell him so.

Such a commitment makes me willing to serve as a volunteer to help stuff envelopes for church mailings. It helps me understand the necessity for committees and councils (and why, perhaps, I should serve on one of them). It gets me to church on Thursday evenings for choir practice, Wednesday evening for Bible study, and up a little earlier on Sunday morning to teach or attend Sunday school. It helps me to wipe the dust off my trumpet or guitar tucked away in the closet and offer to play it for church meetings. It pushes my hand toward my wallet when it comes time to give an offering. It makes it possible for me to drive across town to bring someone to the center of worship. It gives me the desire to want my friends and family in on "the church." This commitment helps me when I get discouraged and keeps me around when people move too slowly for me to appreciate.

You will discover many ways to become an integral part of the church as this commitment becomes a reality in your life. Commitment to Christ means commitment to His church. Without your commitment the church is alive, but you are dead.

TIMING

Timing and patience are crucial. If you are like me, you want things to happen right now, not later. And who has the patience to be patient when it doesn't happen "right now"?

God's timing is perfect. In the creation of the physical world, in the creation of our physical bodies, in the sending of His Son, God's timing is perfect.

Similarly, successful plugging into your church will depend much on your sensitivity to timing—God's timing. Do you want to be more actively involved in your church? Ask God to give you His sensitivity to the needs of your congregation. He will show you when and how your gifts can best be used.

Do you feel your church needs to change the style of worship, teaching, methods, concern for social issues, youth ministry, evangelism, and music (just to name a few)? Then speak up! Ask to be appointed to appropriate committees. Meet with your pastor. Talk to the council members or elders. Suggest alternatives. Run for office. But do whatever you do after:

1. You pray about it. Remember, God answers prayer.

2. You demonstrate your love for your church through your faithfulness, commitment, and helpfulness.

3. You have determined that it is the right time.

Bad timing backfires. Good timing is respected by man and honored by God. Good timing means that we are patient. When you apply the rule of love to your time, the result will be patience. Plugging in means plugging along patiently.

STICK-TO-IT-TIVE-NESS

Faithfulness. If you're going to plug in, plug in, and stay plugged in! What happens when you plug an electrical appliance into the wall socket? After a few minutes the coffee percolates, the toast pops up, the eggs fry, the refrigerator gets cold, the heater warms up. The results don't always come instantly. We learn to keep the cord plugged in for best results.

A valid criticism of church members (young and

74

old) today is that they are fickle, not faithful. As Christians we must exemplify faithfulness to the church; *both the universal body of believers and your local* congregation.

I know people who move from church to church, fellowship to fellowship, whenever they feel the "spirit" leading them. They become anti-institutional, anti-denominational. Pretty soon they get together with a few others like themselves and establish another institution, but before long they become dissatisfied and move again. These people need to learn what *faithfulness* means. We need to be faithful even when we disagree with the way something is done or the way an issue is handled.

Hang in there! Don't give up. Our parents were faithful to us when we had to be fed, led, and changed. If you want to plug into your church, be that kind of faithful—in attendance, consistency in witness, and availability.

AVAILABILITY

Available. Are you? Are we really available to be plugged into the church with its big opportunities and big problems? Have you said, "God, use me anyway you want; use me any place you want." Our availability shouldn't be based on our getting recognition or praise. We should be available for the small, unglorious jobs as well as the glorious ones. In the church availability, more than ability is the key.

The church of Jesus Christ involves both *doing* and *being*. We are called out to imitate who Christ is and follow where Christ goes. This will result in our always being plugged into His church. Christ is the head of his church, and if we are "in Christ" then we will be plugged in where it really counts.

Dick Klawitter

Bible Study— Alone and Together

The setting: Contemporary Problems Class. Jim is speaking. "You know, I'm finding that the Bible has answers for today's problems."

The teacher says: "Jim, I believe the Bible is just a compilation of old hand-me-down stories. Whenever I read it, I get bewildered, confused, and all mixed up. It's not real."

Jim responded: "Sir, the Bible is God's love letter to Christians. That's what you get for reading other people's mail."

Humorous? Possibly. But so true. The Bible tells us about such a situation. In 1 Corinthians 1:18 the Apostle Paul says, *"I know very well how foolish it sounds to those who are lost when they hear that Jesus died to save them. But we who are saved recognize this message as the very power of God"* LB. And again in 1 Corinthians 2:14 Paul talks about a similar situation, *"The man who isn't a Christian can't under-*

stand what the Holy Spirit means. Others just can't take it in" LB.

Why do I share this opening with you? Because I want you to know that since you have decided to live your life with Jesus, the Bible, which was once foolishness to you, will now take on a new exciting dimension. You will realize how the Holy Spirit really does teach us through the Bible.

I would like to share with you some of the principles of Bible study I have found helpful when I study the Scripture with others.

BEGIN WITH PRAYER

As we began our Bible study times together, we found it beneficial to spend some time as a group in conversational prayer. God used this prayer time to lead us into his presence in a fresh way, usually praying out loud, sometimes silently. Following our half-hour of prayer, we would spend another half-hour singing songs of praise, worship, and testimony. We mix in words of witness about what Jesus is doing in our lives, hang-ups we've hassled with, sorrows and burdens we need help with, and many times ending up with prayer for specific needs of our group. This is a good preparation for the study of the Bible.

DECIDE WHAT TO STUDY

You'll have to decide what you're going to study. Do you want to study a topic or a book of the Bible? I suggest that you begin by studying Colossians, written by the Apostle Paul and 1 John, written by the Apostle John. These books give precise, easy-to-apply guidance for Christian living.

EIGHT HELPS IN BIBLE STUDY

After you've decided what to study, then move ahead with the following:

1. **Pray** that the Holy Spirit will open the eyes of your spirit and mind so you can learn what you need to know to be more like Jesus. We would see Jesus!

2. **Look up the background information** on what you're studying: Who wrote it? Who was it written to? When was it written? Why was it written? Where was it written? Locate places on a map. Answers to these questions will be a big help in gaining a better understanding of your study. Use notes, helps, and maps from your Bible, another study Bible, or a Bible handbook.

3. **Read through the entire book** to gain a "feel" of the message. Do this in one sitting. This is important. Seek to concentrate and observe what is being said. (It will help to read it in several different translations and paraphrased Bibles.)

4. Read it through again, this time **make note of a general theme as well as specific themes** for sections or paragraphs. Note key verses and key words. Note verses you'd like to memorize and spend special time meditating on them.

5. **List your section or paragraph themes** or titles and write a brief summary or paraphrase in your own words. This will help you remember the content.

6. **Make a list of the problems or questions** which come to you as you read and paraphrase. Ask yourself, what does the writer really mean? Interpret his message for those to whom he wrote it. Does it mean the same for me today?

7. **How can I apply this message** to my life with Jesus? Do I need to change or refocus my thought life? My goals in life? My actions? My attitudes? My priorities? My values? Should I ask forgiveness of someone I've wronged? Does it point to sin in my life? Does it motivate or challenge me in relationships or responsibilities? Can I claim it as a promise? Am I willing to face up to these questions or applications? Write out these questions of application, or make up your own list, so that they are before you as you study God's Word. Learn them. They will always be a guide as you read and study God's Word.

8. **Learn to use the cross references and concordance** in your Bible. Have someone help you. You will then be able to use these tools to see how one verse agrees with, and supports other verses elsewhere in the Bible.

These suggested steps can be used by an individual or by a small group. You can easily assign different members of the study group to develop the study on one or two paragraphs. Or you can divide the study group into groups of two, three, or more and give them about 15-20 minutes to study the assigned section. They would then share their findings with the entire group. This will be a rich fellowship in Bible Study. Not *foolishness,* but a rewarding *feasting* on God's abundant blessings.

Marge Wold | # Women in the Church

The following events would have made headlines if newspapers had existed in Jesus' time:

JESUS COMMISSIONS A WOMAN TO BE FIRST RESURRECTION PREACHER!
(John 20:11-18; Matthew 28:9-10; Mark 16:1-10)

DISCIPLES CONFOUNDED BY JESUS' FIRST REVELATION OF HIM-SELF AS PROMISED MESSIAH—TO A WOMAN!
(John 4:25-26)

JESUS REJECTS RITUAL UNCLEANNESS OF WOMEN!
(Mark 5:25-34; see Leviticus 5:25-27)

JESUS REBUKES BUSY HOUSEWIFE; PRAISES SISTER WHO CHOOSES INTELLECTUAL ROLE!
(Luke 10:38-42)

JESUS SUPPORTED BY WOMEN FOLLOWERS!
(Mark 15:40-41)

JESUS CHAMPIONS HARLOT IN OPPOSITION TO PHARISEES!
(John 8:3-11; see also Leviticus 20:10)

JESUS SCORNS "ANATOMY IS DESTINY" ROLE FOR WOMEN: CHALLENGES MOTHERHOOD AS HIGHEST IDEAL!
(Luke 11:27-28)

JESUS BEGAN A LIBERATING MOVEMENT
IN THE CHURCH

What feelings are aroused in you by these evidences that Jesus promoted the liberation of women in His day? Does this thought make you feel upset? Proud? Angry? Like celebrating?

There's no denying the fact that Jesus challenged the inferior status to which women were condemned by the Judaic culture. The virtuous Jews of his time felt that it demeaned them to speak with a woman, even with their own wives and daughters. It's no wonder then that the disciples, as we are told in John 4:27, "marveled that he was talking with a woman," when they found Him discussing deep theological subjects with the Samaritan woman at the well! They must have found it very hard to believe that Jesus would risk rabbinic scorn just to make one woman aware of her value as a person.

The playboy image, all beauty queen affirmations of women as "body," the "man-pleaser" identity,—all are denied by Jesus in the beautiful consideration He gave to prostitutes and adulteresses. He refused to be trapped into treating women as sex objects,—"chicks," "bunnies," "whistle-bait," and the like.

On the other hand, Jesus certainly did not sentimentalize motherhood as women's great fulfillment of the will of God for her life. Instead, He seemed to go out of His way to deny the validity of that notion. When a woman called out to Him, piously extolling Mary for her biological female functions (Luke 11:27), Jesus responded, *"Blessed rather are those who hear the word of God and keep it!"*

Another view of women, as it is promoted and glorified by TV commercials, women's magazines, and most preachers, is that of woman as a wildly dedicated housekeeper ("Woman's place is in the home"). In this role she is portrayed as finding ultimate fulfillment in the gleaming wax on her kitchen floor, and as being moved to mad ecstasy by the whiteness of her wash! The unbiblical adage "cleanliness is next to godliness" becomes her creed and her motivating life force. Jesus really chops this "model housewife" role to bits when He rebukes Martha for being so involved in her housework, and instead praises Mary for adopting the religious and intellectual role traditionally reserved in Judaism for men.

In view of the fact that Jesus even issued a call to the church of the future not to take away this theologically oriented role from all the future "Marys" who would pursue it (see Luke 10:42), it's very difficult to understand the subjugation of women which has been practiced by the organized church through the centuries since His resurrection. Women have been placed in the same powerless state as children and slaves in Christian church history, with little change in status from the rabbinical suppression which held them captive in Jesus' day.

IS JESUS' REDEMPTION A LOST CAUSE FOR WOMEN?

If not, then why do most of the articles dealing with the role of the Christian woman still define her in terms of Genesis 3, which deals with the results of the fall into sin? Do hierarchical church structures deny everything Jesus affirmed for women and place her once again in a pre-redeemed state, doomed forever under the curse of the Fall? Paul so beautifully affirmed a Christian woman's liberation in Galatians 3:28, "There is neither Jew nor Greek, there is neither slave nor free, *there is neither male nor female; for you are all one in Christ Jesus.*" Was he later unable to withstand the pressures of tradition as he sought to establish a church in the Hebrew culture? Is that why he seems to contradict himself in 1 Corinthians 11? After discussing cultural role distinctions in the first section of that chapter, he is forced to admit in the 11th verse that *"in the Lord,"* these distinctions do not exist.

IN THE LORD, WOMEN AND MEN ARE EQUAL

At this point, let's check the Creation accounts in Genesis 1 and 2. For instance, there's Genesis 1:27. Is any difference in rank implied in this verse? Apparently not, since both male and female were created in God's image and both were given the same original status in their dominion over the earth and in the reproductive role.

Now look at the somewhat different account in Genesis 2. There woman is designated as man's "helper." How that word has been misused in the subjugation of women! Did you know that the Hebrew word for "helper," *ezer,* never means "assistant" or an inferior person? It is used 21 times in the Old Testament, and 16 times it means the empowering helper, the one who helps another one who is helpless or in distress. Remember all those psalms where the psalmist calls upon God to "help" him? That's the same Hebrew word as the word used for woman as "helper." Doesn't really imply a *lower* rank, does it?

83

AND WHATEVER HAPPENED TO WOMEN
AFTER PENTECOST?

Pentecost was the great Liberation Day for all people, if the prophecy of Joel can be believed. Can it? Or shall we just continue to ignore the fact that the Spirit was poured out on "all flesh,

and your sons *and your daughters* shall prophesy,
and your young men shall see visions,
and your old men shall dream dreams;
yea, and on my menservants *and my maidservants* in those days I will pour out my Spirit; and they shall prophesy." (Acts 2:17-18).

Liberation for the young! Liberation for women! Liberation for slaves! Loosened tongues, community concern and shared resources (Acts 2:44-45), a breaking down of hierarchical structures! The gifts and the fruits of the Spirit available to every person in the Christian community!

SO WHERE DO WE GO FROM HERE?

1. Women need to be helped to see themselves as fully redeemed human beings, and therefore free to follow their liberating Lord wherever He calls them.

2. Both men and women need to be freed from cultural role stereotypes which squeeze us all into the world's mold, instead of allowing us to be transformed into the image of Christ. Pastors can help by pointing to Jesus' freeing statements and behavior as the context in which all other reference to women's "place" must be interpreted.

3. Creation and the Church can only be "whole" when both men and women of all races and all ages

and all socio-economic classes work together in a loving relationship as "one in Christ" and therefore "one in the Spirit," claiming again their pre-Fall relationship to God and to each other.

4. Young men and young women must work together to establish a new spirit of mutuality between the sexes; as partners in the gospel, they must deny the validity of the "authority-submission" patterns and live as *"subject to one another out of reverence of Christ"* (Ephesians 5:21).

Rod Rosenbladt

How Do I Share My Faith?

The Christian who takes the Scriptures seriously is often confronted with the command to be a *witness*. The Scriptures tell us that this has to do with presenting Jesus Christ to those who have not yet come to know Him. A Christian witness is basically one who testifies concerning the person and work of Jesus Christ.

But, as we all know, this is more easily said than done. I remember directing a training session in evangelism for a church board. I began by asking, "What are the two hardest words to utter in a social situation?" A lawyer fired back, "Jesus Christ." He was right—at least as far as most of us are concerned. Many have tried gritting their teeth and venturing to speak of the Gospel, only to come away as Paul Little says, "unnerved as an elephant on ice."

James Kennedy tells the story of a salesman who went with him to observe an evangelism call. The man called the next morning to tell Dr. Kennedy that he vomited as soon as he returned to his house! Must communicating Christ cause this kind of panic? Not really, if the testimony of many Christians today is any indicator. Evangelism is an art which *can* be learned. With practice, we can actually become relatively comfortable doing it. Of course you and I aren't Billy Graham—but that isn't the point. *Doing* evangelism is not the same as being *called* to it or *gifted* with it.

WHAT WE NEED TO KNOW

Where does one begin? The starting place is a working knowledge of the gospel. Notice I did *not* say a working knowledge of the whole Bible. (New Christians have been known to lead others to a saving relationship with Christ before they knew Moses existed!) What must one know?

1. He must know how God created man good and in perfect personal relationship to Himself.

2. He must understand what sin is: a disease deep within every man causing him to rebel toward his Creator.

3. He must know how sin separates God and man.

4. He must possess a basic knowledge of God's character or attributes—at least holiness and love.

5. Most important of all, he ought to be able to verbalize the meaning of Jesus Christ for man's problem—especially His substitutionary death for our sin.

6. Finally, he must be able to explain how God plans for a person to share in the salvation purchased by Christ. God has arranged that we receive salvation by faith. (Note: flee any definition of "faith" which implies that it is "blind" or anti-intellectual!)

A biblically-buttressed knowledge of these themes should enable one to lead non-Christians to a saving knowledge of Christ.

BUT I'M SCARED

What about the fright inherent in witnessing? Initially, it is of great help to be a part of a supportive group engaged in evangelism. A supportive group can encourage and enable us to do what we could never do alone. Strong relational ties, prayer for one another, and discussion of problems can help cases of the jitters tremendously. Much failure in the field of evangelism can be traced directly to the lack of support. If fright is your problem, consider a small-group experiment such as Richard Peace's *Witness* (Zondervan).

With practice, we can become less and less uncomfortable when engaged in evangelism. This is essential. If we clutch, the non-Christian senses our uptightness and clutches with us. Probably the best corrective to this is to observe someone who is comfortable presenting the gospel. It is much easier to duplicate what we have actually seen done. The goal is to be able to present Jesus Christ as comfortably as we talk about what interests us in other areas of our lives (skindiving, creative writing, or a new car).

The ease with which we do this depends to a great degree on how much regular contact we have with non-Christians! It is all too easy for the Christian to suddenly wake up to the fact that he no longer has any non-Christian friends. The longer we remain isolated in church circles, the more difficult it will be to comfortably present the gospel to unbelievers.

ARE "EVANGELISM HELPS" HELPFUL?

What about pre-planned gimmicks? What reliance should be made upon aids such as "The Four Spiritual Laws" or the "A,B,C's of Life"? This is a difficult question to answer. For most people contemplating evangelism, an aid can be of tremendous help. Booklets or memorized outlines give a person confidence in guiding the conversation and keeping it on the subject of Christ. In the long run, however, I think we should be able to discern where our listeners are by means of their conversation. Then, knowing the message of the gospel well, we can fit a presentation to that particular person. If we can arrive at this point of proficiency, fewer of our audience will have the idea that they have been "processed."

CHRISTIAN APOLOGETICS

Lastly, an area all too often overlooked which has a direct relationship to evangelism: Christian apologetics. (It refers to a reasoned defense of the gospel as truth—not apologizing for it!) It is tremendously freeing to know that what you are presenting is real truth and not just another helpful religious experience. Apologetic knowledge also helps you to field those few questions that constantly recur during evangelistic activity ("What about the sincere Buddhist?" "How could a loving God allow war and genetic defects?" "Hasn't science disproved the possibility of miracles?")

At the end of this article is a list of some books which may be helpful in answering questions like these—both for yourself and when explaining the Christian faith to others. Any reading you can do in these apologetic books will be beneficial to you in evangelism.

Books on Witnessing

Harding, B. "The Content of the Gospel" (HIS Magazine reprint)

Kennedy, D. James. *Evangelism Explosion* (Tyndale House)

Little, Paul. *How to Give Away Your Faith* (Inter-Varsity Press)

Stott, John R. *Basic Christianity (Eerdmans), Our Guilty Silence* (Eerdmans)

Books on Apologetics

Bruce, F. F. *The New Testament Documents: Are They Reliable?* (Eerdmans)

Lewis, C. S. *Mere Christianity* (MacMillan)

Little, Paul. *Know Why You Believe* (Inter-Varsity Press)

Montgomery, John Warwick. *History and Christianity* (Inter-Varsity Press)

What Can I Do to Be a Missionary?

Paul J. Lindell

There are some basic qualifications that ought to be a part of the equipment of any missionary, whoever you are, wherever you go, and whatever you do.

1. **Get to know Jesus Christ personally.** This is the place to start. Jesus came into the world to save sinners from their sins, from the evil power of the devil and from "the wrath to come," i.e., from the final judgment of God upon all who are yet in their sins (Matthew 3:7; Colossians 3:5-6). And the first and primary work of missions is to make known to all people the good news about Jesus as the Savior of the world.

You are and always will be a sinner, as long as you live in this world. Your own case is hopeless unless you know Jesus as your Savior. You cannot tell another sinner the way to peace with God unless you are living in God's gracious forgiveness through Jesus Christ. The Scripture says, "He who has the Son has life; he who has not the Son has not life" (1 John 5:12 RSV).

Thus, until you know Jesus Christ and live and walk with him, it will be useless to think of being his missionary.

2. **Get a clear call from God.** One striking mark that was common to the Apostle Paul, John the Baptist, Moses, King David, and even Jesus is that God called and sent them. They, and others like them, did what they did because God told them to do it.

This sense of being called and sent by God comes to people in different ways. When it is genuine, the Holy Spirit sustains his call with persistent assurances all through the years.

Look for God's call and leading to you. Let it come in God's own way, and then treasure it as a most precious gift and trust from God to you.

3. **Get a broad view of the Christian mission.** Many missionaries fail to do this. They see only their own place of work and miss the joy of being swept along in the full tide of God's mission in the whole world.

You will have to work and study to get a broad view. Read all you can about the history of missions since the time of Christ. Go to missionary conferences, study missionary magazines and reports. Talk to missionaries. Ask questions. Take notes. Discuss what you learn with others who have the same interest as you have. And determine to work at this for the rest of your life.

4. **Get filled with the Word of God.** Your tool chest, your medicine bag, your textbook, your road map is the Bible. Know your way around in the Bible, forwards and backwards. Get hold of its contents, its teachings, its mind and mood and spirit.

Treat it always with humility, with faith and with expectation. Let it master your conscience, mind, and

92

heart. It is the means God uses to bring saving grace to people. It is the meeting place with God.

5. **Get to know the world.** A Christian missionary, more than anyone else, should want to know all he can about the world. This is because he has been taken into the love that God has for all men and for the earth that God has made to be their home.

Be always a learner. Be everlastingly curious and inquisitive. Ask questions. Open up your eyes and ears and mind to all you can discover about this complex, wonderful, fearful world. This world is what Jesus called our "field" (John 4:35). As a good farmer carefully tends his field, so a good missionary will diligently study and cultivate his world.

6. **Get a skill.** Learn a trade. Qualify in a profession. Learn to do something useful, something by which you can serve and help other people. Don't be halfhearted about this, and don't stop at half measures. If you decide to be a nurse, a teacher, a librarian, a social worker, a bookkeeper, a preacher, or a hostess for a mission home and headquarters in some foreign land, then get the best training you can and give it all you've got.

7. **Get into an active Christian fellowship.** The Christian's faith and life in Christ are intensely personal, but they are not private. They are corporate. And this is true also of his service under Christ's power and authority.

In 1 Corinthians 12:12-27 Paul says that each member of the body cannot function alone, but only as one of many parts in the body. Also, each member cannot act purposefully alone, but only in concert with the other members of the body.

Don't think you can get along without the fellowship of others. Don't think that just attending church services and then going home is all the fellowship you need. And don't think that getting active in organizations and programs with other college students, or with young people in your church is what is meant by spiritual fellowship. If this is all you have, you won't last long as a missionary.

8. **Get Rid of everything that gets in the way** (Hebrews 12:1). That's a big order and it sometimes takes quite a while for a missionary to discover what is holding him down and keeping him back from doing his best on the job. But you can save yourself a lot of grief later on by learning now how to clean out and get rid of what is useless to you as Christ's servant. Think over these suggestions:

A. Get rid of your pride and prejudices. A few years ago someone wrote a book called *The Ugly American,* showing how Americans look to people in other nations. They see Americans as proud, loud-mouthed, prejudiced, selfish, boastful, impatient, unwilling to listen and learn. We must get rid of those attitudes that make us look *ugly* to others.

B. Get rid of your critical attitudes. You probably have some of this. We all do. I notice that high school and college folks generally have lots of it—towards each other, toward their parents, pastor, church, school and most anybody. They talk people down and not up. If you can't dump this stuff off and get rid of it, you will be one miserable missionary some day.

C. Get rid of unnecessary possessions and learn to live without much that other people regard as necessary. I have a big bagful of stories about the troubles and losses that missionaries have had with their possessions. These stories all end up with the same firm advice: keep and hold only such things as you need for your work, and even these things should be held with a light hand, for you may lose them any time.

Hudson Taylor, the pioneer missionary to China, is said to have made an inventory of his books and other belongings once a year. Over each item he asked the question: "Is this necessary for the work God has given me to do?" If the answer was "No," he got rid of it.

D. Get rid of entertainment. Oh, not all of it, but about 90% of it anyway. America is flooded with entertainment. Movies, radio, TV, books, magazines, and even advertising are all designed to entertain the American. And we fall for it. Our spare time between college classes or work shifts and our evenings are surrendered to entertainment. It's taken for granted. We don't think to question it.

But if you go to live with poor people and to be the servant of Christ among them in some yonder village or tribe, you will leave almost all of this behind. Better start dumping a lot of it now or you will have a hard time of it later.

9. **Get love.** Get it for real. *"Let love be genuine,"* says Paul in the New Testament (Romans 12:9). Evidently there is spurious love, only pretended, and this does no good.

The love the Bible talks about is not something emotional. Love is convictional (2 Corinthians 5:14). Love is an attitude that leads to action. No doubt feelings and emotions will play a part because we are made up that way. But basically love is an attitude. Love means to have God's attitude towards all other people.

God commands us to love our fellow men. Now if love were merely an emotion or feeling it could not be commanded, for you cannot require a certain emotion in someone else. But you can demand that there be a particular attitude. And this is what God does when He tells us to love one another, even our enemies!

God is love and love comes from God, says the Apostle John (1 John 4:7-8). The nature of this love is displayed in Jesus. It is merciful, forgiving, redemptive, healing. God acts that way, always, and His attitude and His saving deeds are called love.

10. **And now get going.** Get going on all of this right now, today, right where you are. Crossing an ocean won't make you a missionary. Getting an advanced university degree won't make you a missionary. But if you get going now with what I have been saying, in your home and on your campus, you will be Christ's missionary starting today. And later on when the Holy Spirit sends you off to some other corner of the world you will be ready for it, an experienced missionary, and what you meet will not seem strange to you at all.

God bless you. Carry on in the strength that comes from God.

Nelson Trout | Me? Prejudiced?

Prejudice infiltrates and infects us all. If you are white, you have been victimized by a whole set of circumstances which contrive to make you prejudiced against most minorities in the United States. And if you belong to a minority, you have been victimized by another whole set of circumstances which contrive to make you prejudiced against most whites.

The word *prejudice* suggests that we relate to people of another race with *too little information* and also, most certainly, with false information. Relationships built on such shaky foundations are sure to be prejudiced.

The society in which we live gives massive evidence that racial prejudice is actively at work. For example, to be born white in America is to be born with a set of assumptions which are not a part of the black experience.

One who is born non-white in America soon learns

to live defensively. He discovers that his humanity is not assumed. His worth as a person is questioned. And at every point in his life he must justify his existence. To be the victim of this kind of prejudice is to experience existential absurdity—life doesn't make sense.

HOW PREJUDICE LIVES

Prejudice feeds on itself. This is evident in the passion of parents to pass their prejudices on to their children. With great subtlety, prejudice affects the lives of the innocent. A child brought up in an allegedly Christian home can be infected with racial prejudice without knowing it.

It is difficult to differentiate between the prejudices which we learn and all our other learning. Unfortunately, it also takes a long time to sit in judgment on our own prejudices. This is like lifting ourselves by our own bootstraps. Usually by the time we learn that we are prejudiced, the reality is so mixed up with our thoughts and feelings that it becomes virtually impossible to free ourselves from it.

THE RESULTS OF PREJUDICE

Prejudice in race relations is responsible for a great deal of hurt in our society. It is accompanied by our stubborn insensitivity to the harm which we may inflict against another. You can see it in the eyes that look at you. That exchange of glances is not the recognition of one human being by another. It is the look of arrogance, stripping another human being of his God-given humanity. And you can hear prejudice in the voice of one who has a false notion of his own importance as he addresses another creature whom he feels to be beneath his station.

A CALL TO CHRISTIANS

I appeal to all young Christians who are concerned about bringing healing to our society by saying that racial prejudice is essentially a tragedy. When human beings confront each other, there should be recognition and celebration. Instead too often there is denial and disapproval. This tragedy occurs all over this land. It occurs in all walks of life. It occurs in every phase of human endeavor.

The church, you would think, is finding ways to alleviate the problem. Regrettably, this is not generally true. The church knows what the Scriptures say but is unable to translate what the Scriptures say into the lifestyles of enough of its people. Martin Luther King said that the most segregated hour of the week was 11:00 on Sunday morning.

Young Christians, resolve that with you the Word of Life will be given a new opportunity to speak to men and women concerning the way they look on each other. Surely the honesty and integrity which characterizes so much of youth culture today, combined with the Christian message of brotherly love will find every authentic young Christian an advocate for change in the whole area of race relations.

You could bring to silence the sirens of despair. You could point us again to the meaning of the incarnation: namely, that it was God becoming man so that each of us may find our worth in His becoming one with us. Because of Christ's identification with us it is unbecoming for any of us to look with disdain

upon another of us. Our Christian faith teaches us that God is no respecter of persons (Acts 10:34).

The gospel of Jesus Christ is all about freedom, liberation, wholeness, peace, and joy. As we find our partnership in the gospel, may we also find each other (Matthew 11:5-6).

Ours is a pluralistic society. God has created his world with cosmic diversity. In fact it is apparent as we look about us that God has a passion for diversity. He allows for diversity both in nature and in human nature. As for men: some are white, some are black, some are yellow, some are brown, and some are red. Some have straight hair, some have curly hair, some have kinky hair; some have big lips, some have thin lips. They come in all shapes and sizes. Why should we accentuate our differences in such a way that these differences become barriers separating us from each other? Young Christian, I issue a challenge to you: teach us how to celebrate our differences, to the honor and glory of God.

What Do I Owe My Country?

Charles P. Lutz

Do I owe my country anything?

Everyone does, of course—if by "country" we mean the society, the set of institutions, the governmental system one was born into or has adopted.

The tough question is: how much do I owe that country, or how far do I go before my allegiance legitimately ends?

As a Christian, I begin by reminding myself that there are higher allegiances. My first—and final—allegiance is to the God who creates me, redeems me in Jesus Christ, and lives in me through His Spirit. That means, obviously, if there is conflict between what my country asks of me and what I understand God to be asking of me, I follow the latter.

I have another allegiance which has claim on me ahead of my country. It is my identification with fellow believers throughout the world. My citizenship in the People of God comes ahead of my citizenship in any particular nation.

And for many Christians (myself included), loyalty to the world community—our common humanity with mankind everywhere—also comes ahead of loyalty to the political entity in which one was born or holds citizenship.

The Scriptures teach that the meaning of history is borne, not by the United States or any other nation, not even by Western Christendom, but by a divine-human community, the church, the Body of Christ. That community is a *supra*-national one. When Christians endorse the aims of any one nation in a way that leads them to do violence against fellow Christians in another nation, great offense against the unity of Christ's body takes place. St. Paul reminds us that it is already a unity that includes *all men:* through the Cross, Christ creates "a *single new humanity in himself, thereby making peace*" (Ephesians 2:15 NEB).

THREE COUNSELS

Speaking broadly, there are three sorts of biblical counsel concerning an individual's relationship to his government.

The first, represented by Acts 5:29, we have just discussed briefly. It is the assertion that God's will comes ahead of what men require of us, whenever there is a conflict between the two. "*We must obey God rather than men.*"

A second sort of counsel is stated most clearly in Romans 13:1, "*Let every person be subject to the governing authorities.*" Christians have usually taken this to mean that the *institution* of government is legitimate—and in the normal flow of daily life its laws and procedures should be accepted, with changes coming

102

about through peaceable and orderly means. When we read Romans 13, we usually think of national governing authorities, since it is nations today which have the most power and authority, politically. But we should remind ourselves that the nation-state we know today is a fairly new development, since the time of biblical writings. Romans 13 also implies obedience to other levels of governing authority, such as international law, the principles of war crimes tribunals (like Nuremburg), actions voted by the United Nations, and other international agreements or conventions.

A third biblical word about sovereign political authority is expressed most clearly in Revelation 13. There, we are warned about government's tendency to become absolute in its claims, to want to become God. The writer was undoubtedly speaking of the Roman Empire and the emperor himself, but it is a reality known also in our time. And the tendency is there with every government, even the most democratic and benevolent—to require absolute allegience when only relative allegiance is appropriate. Often, the idolatry is most noticeable at times of international conflict.

THREE DEBTS

If it is clear that I owe my country a great deal less than absolute loyalty, what do I owe? I would list three debts.

First, I owe my country a *life that is useful*. I owe it my service as a contributing member of the society. I don't owe service to an abstraction called "nation," nor even to a national government. I owe my service to the people of my country, to my neighbors. If I am an American, most of my opportunities to serve will be among other Americans. But sometimes, as with the Peace Corps, my national government may be the vehicle by which I may serve neighbors in other countries.

Another thing I owe my country is *the courage to dissent* when I believe she is taking a wrong course. This is another way of saying that true patriotism includes the possibility of having to say "no" to what my government asks of me.

Henry David Thoreau, a patriot who often dissented in the America of over 100 years ago, believed his government was wrong in prosecuting the Mexican War. In stating his objection, he observed: "A very few men serve the State with their consciences, and they are commonly treated as enemies by it." Thoreau saw those who refused to do the law's bidding for reasons of conscience as serving their country in a most admirable and necessary way.

America has a long history of dissent, with people going to jail as a protest against laws they considered unjust. Laws upholding enslavement of other human beings, forbidding the organizing of labor unions, prohibiting distribution of information about human reproduction, requiring pacifists to serve in the military —you can make your own list. In all these cases, the laws have later been changed, and the witness of the dissenting minority was a key to that change.

Finally, I owe my country *a vision which is global.* Nationalism—devotion only to the interests of a particular nation—is no service to my country. Nationalism is a form of idolatry, because it believes my country cannot err. It wants always to make my country's interests the measurement of what is best, without concern for the rest of mankind.

I owe my country a bigger vision, one that will make my country a blessing to all the earth, one that asks my country to give of herself in bringing justice and peace everywhere. If I live in the world's most powerful country, I owe my country the demand that she become number one in waging peace.

What do I owe my country? I owe my country patriotism—wanting the best for her, which is not the same as thinking she is best, no matter what she does.

As a patriot, and as a Christian, I owe my country the service of a useful occupation.

As a patriot, and as a Christian, I owe my country the courage of dissent when I believe she is following a wrong course.

As a patriot, and as a Christian, I owe my country my insistence that she use her power to be a blessing to the world.

Carl Johansson

How to Face the Future

When we study the Bible, we find that God's Spirit wants to teach us about the future, our future. And it's all centered around the second coming of Jesus Christ. The second coming of Jesus and the final wrap-up of history is priority in the Bible. John says to have ears. Look what Jesus says in Matthew 24:3-51. Rapid fire, He says, *men can fool you;* then, *no one knows;* followed by the picture, *it is like a thief;* accompanied by parables of creative expectancy, parables of grace and judgment.

The Apostle Peter takes up the theme in 2 Peter 3:3-15. He says, be ready for the flack when God does not produce according to human time tables. God's timetable is not in terms of the calendar but in terms of response. It is *kairos* (God's view of time), not *"chronos"* (man's calendar time). Peter goes on to say that God's wrap-up of time is in terms of blowing the whole bit up like a "nova." He concludes the section by talking about the evangelistic implications of living in view of God's deadline. Peter says, in view of Christ's second coming we ought to live zealous, holy, righteous lives.

God's Spirit speaks through Paul in 1 Thessalonians 5:1-11. He stresses the thief image again, suggesting that we ought to be in expectancy constantly with its resultant implications of a style of life.

FIVE MIND-BLOWING TRUTHS

From Scripture we find five truths that revolutionize our lives.

1. Jesus is coming again. He is the Lord of history and geography, but eminently of people who are more important to Him than either. So ecology and time-tables take second place to His recycling of persons and of creation through death and resurrection.

2. The second coming of Christ cannot be charted on a human calendar because it is based on God's evaluation of human response (kairos)—not on a rigid pattern of history (chronos).

3. Therefore, from our point of view the coming of Christ is pictured as a thief, a blow-up, lightning across the skies.

4. God can wrap up all creation before you have finished reading this sentence. That's what we mean when the Bible speaks of God's imminence.

5. This has evangelistic implications and social implications. We hang loose as a style of life. All that we do for Jesus Christ in this passing world has continuity

in on-going life climaxed in a new heavens and a new earth where righteousness is at home.

Time is God's turf for you and me to achieve His purposes. Its dimensions are not measured by days or years, but by how God's purposes are achieved in our lives and in our world.

THREE CLUES FOR OUR DAY

There is a bridge to our basic stance of being radical Christians in today's world. There are three words stemming from the acronym **EAR.** They are what we hear when we listen in our day with a biblical frame of reference and a Christ-honoring purpose. They are clues in our day. The first word is **eschatological.** It is translated in the Bible as: final, last, total, complete, uttermost, extreme, ultimate. When you summarize the biblical meaning, it comes out like this:

1. God has a final wrap-up that is judgment—ultimate eschatology.

2. God has historical and cultural times of judgment that become the watershed of cultures, churches, eras and civilizations.

3. God has personal eschatological times in this life that will either mean judgment or grace to you.

4. The Christian should take each day as an eschatological entity. And instead of "sunrise" and "sunset," it becomes to him "Sonrise" and "Sonset."

5. What we do with the eschatological possibility of each day determines what it will mean to us, to our lost world, and to Jesus Christ.

The second part of **EAR** is **apocalyptic.** Its various translations are: revealed, manifested, lighten, revelation, coming, appearing, shown, uncovered. In the final (eschatological) time, Jesus is revealed. He is apocalypticized. This is always the other side of eschatology.

We can sum up its biblical thrust with the following:

1. The counterpart of final judgment is revealed grace.

2. Jesus is revealed whenever we come to the end of ourselves personally. And this is an on-going experience.

3. This is true corporately.

4. This is true culturally.

5. This is true ultimately.

The last word of **EAR** is **revolutionary.** A revolution is the turn of a wheel around the hub. In our final time, Jesus is revealed in revolutionary terms. We cannot rotate around any other center but the Person of Jesus Christ.

One revolution of any wheel on a car will take you about three-and-a-half feet. The same is true in our lives. That's the only way you can face the future with confidence. Life has meaning now because Christ is here now. The future has meaning because Christ has promised to be the same tomorrow as he is today. If we want to move ahead, we must continually revolve around the hub, Jesus Christ.

Maranatha! Christ is coming soon! The big question is, are you linked to His revolutionary purpose in your life which is already here and has meaning because He is coming soon?

About the Writers

Dave Anderson: Dave recently compiled *Jesus Style Songs Vol. 1.* He is the Director of Youth Ministry, Lutheran Youth Alive, Los Angeles, California.

William Berg: Pastor of Augustana Lutheran Church (LCA), Minneapolis, Minnesota, Dr. Berg has successfully melted together evangelism and social ministry in an urban congregation.

Ken Berven: Christian businessman, lecturer and author of *Blest Be the Tie that Frees,* Ken makes his home in Seattle, Washington.

Don Fladland: Youth evangelist and conference speaker, Don is the Director of Youth Outreach at the Lutheran Bible Institute, Seattle Washington.

Pete Gillquist: Popular lecturer and author of *Love Is Now* and *Farewell to the Fake I.D.,* Peter lives in Grand Junction, Tennessee.

Allan and Eunice Hansen: This couple has opened their home and hearts to youth in crisis. Allan is the director of Renewal House, Lutheran Social Services, Los Angeles, California.

Roy Hendrickson: Formerly Director of Ministry for Lutheran Youth Encounter, Roy is now a pastor in Albert Lea, Minnesota.

Oswald C. J. Hoffmann: International communicator of the gospel, Dr. Hoffmann is the speaker for *The Lutheran Hour.*

Carl Johansson: Missionary to West Africa and former Executive Secretary of the Evangelical Lutheran Church in Tanganyika, Rev. Johansson is pastor of Trinity Evangelical Lutheran Church of Minnehaha Falls (LCA), Minneapolis, Minnesota.

Dick Klawitter: Dick developed one of the most intensive Teen Age Bible Studies (TABS) in Seattle, Washington. He is now the Director of Youth Ministry for the Lutheran Evangelical Movement, Minneapolis, Minnesota.

Paul Lindell: Paul is the Director of the World Mission Prayer League, Minneapolis, Minnesota. Born and reared in China, Paul is a counselor and Bible teacher.

Conrad E. Lund: Formerly a pastor in Seattle, Washington, Reverend Lund is now the president of the Lutheran Bible Institute, Seattle.

Charles Lutz: Now on the ALC staff, Chuck was the director of Lutheran Selective Service Information.

Charles S. Mueller: Author and lecturer, Pastor Mueller is the president of the Southeastern District, Lutheran Church—Missouri Synod.

Robert M. Overgaard: Formerly a pastor in Pasadena, California, Bob Overgaard is the editor of *Faith and Fellowship* and is the executive Secretary of Foreign Missions for the Church of the Lutheran Brethren, Fergus Falls, Minnesota.

Cliff Pederson: Cliff served two Lutheran congregations (LCA) as Director of Youth Ministry while attending college and seminary. He was also the Director of Publications for Gospel Broadcasting Association, producer of *The Joyful Sound* formerly *The Old Fashioned*

Revival Hour. A Bible teacher and conference speaker, Cliff is presently the Director of Adult Ministry for Lutheran Youth Alive, Los Angeles, California.

Alvin N. Rogness: President, Luther Theological Seminary, St. Paul, Minnesota, and author of *The Jesus Life, Signs of Hope in the Thunder of Spring,* and *The Wonder of Being Loved.*

Rod Rosenbladt: Skilled in apologetics and formerly assistant to Paul Little, Rod served as pastor of La Jolla Lutheran Church (ALC), La Jolla, California.

Nelson Trout: Dr. Trout is the Executive Director of Lutheran Social Services, Miami Valley, Dayton, Ohio. He was formerly a pastor and member of the staffs of the American Lutheran Church's Commission on Evangelism and Division of Youth Activity.

Bob Turnbull: Brings the gospel to the beaches of Waikiki, Bob is the President of World Resort Chaplaincies.

Don Williams: New Testament scholar and author of *Call to the Streets,* Don now teaches at Claremont College, California.

Marge Wold: Author and teacher, Marge is the Executive Director of the American Lutheran Church Women, Minneapolis, Minnesota.